RAND

Who Is Joint? Reevaluating the Joint Duty Assignment List

John F. Schank, Harry J. Thie, Jennifer Kawata, Margaret C. Harrell, Clifford M. Graf II, Paul Steinberg

Prepared for the Joint Staff

National Defense Research Institute

Approved for public release; distribution unlimited

Preface

Title IV of the Goldwater-Nichols DoD Reorganization Act of 1986 specified a system of joint officer management, including management policies, promotion objectives, and educational and experience requirements. The intent of the personnel provision was to enhance the quality, stability, and experience of officers in joint assignments (those assignments to organizations outside an officer's individual military service that address issues involving multiple services or other nations), which, in turn, would improve the performance and effectiveness of joint organizations.

In 1987, the Secretary of Defense published a list of joint duty assignment positions. In developing this Joint Duty Assignment List (JDAL), the Secretary limited joint duty positions to officers in the pay grades of O-4 (major, or lieutenant commander in the Navy) and above. All such positions in certain organizations (Office of the Secretary of Defense, the Joint Staff, and the unified commands) and a maximum of 50 percent of defense agency positions were designated as joint duty assignments.

The 1993 National Defense Authorization Act requested a reexamination of the rules implementing the Goldwater-Nichols legislation. The Joint Staff's Director of Manpower and Personnel requested RAND to provide information and analysis to assist in conducting the study mandated by Congress and to evaluate alternative policy choices for the size and composition of the JDAL and for joint officer management. To accomplish this, RAND researchers examined issues on both the demand side and the supply side of officer management. This report describes the results and recommendations of the demand-side analysis. A companion document, MR-593-JS, *How Many Can Be Joint? Supporting Joint Duty Assignments*, describes the results and recommendations of the supply-side analysis.

The research was conducted in the Forces and Resources Policy Center of the National Defense Research Institute, a federally funded research and development center sponsored by the Office of the Secretary of Defense, the Joint Staff, and the defense agencies. The report should be of interest to policymakers and organizations concerned with military (especially joint) officer management.

Contents

Preface iii

Figures vii

Tables ix

Summary xi

Acknowledgments xv

Abbreviations and Acronyms xvii

1. INTRODUCTION 1
   Background 1
   The Goldwater-Nichols Department of Defense Reorganization Act of 1986 1
   Goldwater-Nichols Implementation Concerns 1
   Congressional Directive 2
   Objectives and Approach 3
   Identifying Criteria to Measure Joint Content 4
   Surveying Candidate Billets 5
   Organization of the Report 7

2. CONDUCTING THE DEMAND-SIDE ANALYSIS 8
   Determining Factors for Measuring Joint Content 8
   Preliminary Reviews 8
   Identification of Initial Criteria 10
   Conducting Focus Group Sessions 11
   Determining Final Criteria for Analysis 12
   Combining Criteria to Produce a Joint Score for a Billet 14
   Calculating Scores for the Selected Criteria 14
   Developing Algorithms Combining Scored Criteria 18
   Comparing Results Across the Various Algorithms 19
   Selecting a Preferred Algorithm 20
   Determining the Potential Size of a New JDAL 23
   Cluster Analysis 23
   Other Statistical Techniques 24
   Applying the Techniques 24
   Determining a Potential New JDAL 25

3. IMPLICATIONS OF APPLYING THE JOINT TIME/JOINT FUNCTION ALGORITHM 27
   Implications Under Current Law and DoD Policy 27
   Implications If Current Policy Were Changed to Allow O-3 Billets 30
   Implications If Current Law Were Changed to Allow In-Service Positions 34

Determining the Number of Critical Billets 36
Background 36
A Methodology for Determining the Number of Critical Billets 37

4. CONCLUSIONS AND RECOMMENDATIONS 42
Conclusions 42
Recommendations 43

Appendix
A. OVERVIEW OF GOLDWATER-NICHOLS 45
B. SURVEY QUESTIONNAIRE 53
C. DETAILED RESULTS FROM THE GROUP SESSIONS 67
D. RESULTS OF RESPONSES TO THE SURVEY'S OPINION QUESTIONS 78

Bibliography 95

Figures

2.1. Distribution of Number of Services Score 15
2.2. Distribution of Joint Time Score 16
2.3. Distribution of Joint Function Score 18
2.4. Distribution of Nonjoint Function Score 18
2.5. Results of Algorithm Analysis 20
2.6. Distribution of Joint Scores from Algorithm 2 25
3.1. Percentage of Processed Billets on a JDAL Using Algorithm 2 28
3.2. Percentage of Defense Agency Positions 29
3.3. Number of Positions by Military Service 29
3.4. Number of Positions by Grade 30
3.5. Number of Positions by Selected Skill Group 31
3.6. Number of Positions by Organization Including Grade O-3 32
3.7. Number of Positions on JDAL by Service Including Grade O-3 32
3.8. Number of Positions on JDAL by Skill Group Including Grade O-3 33
3.9. In-Service Positions Added to JDAL by Service 34
3.10. In-Service Positions Added to JDAL by Grade 35
3.11. In-Service Positions Added to JDAL by Skill Group 35
3.12. Critical Billets By Organization 40
3.13. Critical Billets by Service and Grade 41
D.1. Summary of Responses to Opinion Questions 79

Tables

1.1. Survey Responses 6
2.1. Average Criteria Weights from Group Sessions 11
2.2. Average Values for Functional Duties 12
2.3. Average Values for Subject Areas 13
2.4. Size of New JDALs Based on Scoring Algorithm 26
3.1. Size of New JDALs Based on Scoring Algorithm, Including O-3 Billets 31
3.2. Size of New JDALs Based on Scoring Algorithm, Including O-3s and In-Service Billets 34
3.3. Example of Critical Billet Methodology 39
3.4. Effect on Number of Critical Billets of Adjusting Values for Joint Content Variables 40
A.1. Composition of the JDAL by Service and Pay Grade 50
A.2. Critical Joint Positions by Activity 51
C.1. Relative Criteria Weights from J-1 Session 68
C.2. Relative Criteria Weights from Executive Council Session 69
C.3. Relative Criteria Weights from Joint Staff Session 69
C.4. Relative Criteria Weights from Personnel Planner Session 69
C.5. Relative Criteria Weights from Defense Agency Session 70
C.6. Average Criteria Weights from Group Sessions 70
C.7. Calculation of Revised Weights 71
C.8. Duty Values from Executive Council Session 72
C.9. Duty Values from Joint Staff Session 72
C.10. Duty Values from Service Personnel Planner Session 73
C.11. Duty Values from Defense Agency Session 74
C.12. Average Duty Values 75
C.13. Subject Area Values from Group Sessions 76
D.1. Question 19: Responses by Grade 81
D.2. Question 19: Responses by Type Organization 81
D.3. Question 19: Responses by Skill Group 81
D.4. Question 19: Responses by Current Joint Assignment 82
D.5. Question 20: Responses by Grade 82
D.6. Question 20: Responses by Type Organization 82
D.7. Question 20: Responses by Skill Group 83
D.8. Question 20: Responses by Current Joint Assignment 83
D.9. Question 21: Responses by Grade 83
D.10. Question 21: Responses by Type Organization 84
D.11. Question 21: Responses by Skill Group 84
D.12. Question 22: Responses by Grade 84
D.13. Question 22: Responses by Service 85
D.14. Question 22: Responses by Skill 85
D.15. Question 22: Responses by Current Joint Assignment 85
D.16. Question 23: Responses by Grade 86
D.17. Question 23: Responses by Service 86
D.18. Question 23: Responses by Skill Group 86

D.19. Question 23: Responses by Current Joint Assignment 87
D.20. Question 24: Responses by Grade 87
D.21. Question 24: Responses by Service 87
D.22. Question 24: Responses by Skill Group 88
D.23. Question 24: Responses by Current Joint Assignment 88
D.24. Question 25: Responses by Grade 88
D.25. Question 25: Responses by Service 89
D.26. Question 25: Responses by Skill Group 89
D.27. Question 26: Responses by Grade 89
D.28. Question 26: Responses by Service 90
D.29. Question 26: Responses by Skill Group 90
D.30. Question 27: Responses by Grade 90
D.31. Question 27: Responses by Service 91
D.32. Question 27: Responses by Type Organization 91
D.33. Question 27: Responses by Current Joint Assignment 91
D.34. Question 28: Responses by Grade 92
D.35. Question 28: Responses by Service 92
D.36. Question 28: Responses by Skill Group 92
D.37. Question 29: Responses by Grade 93
D.38. Question 29: Responses by Service 93
D.39. Question 29: Responses by Current Joint Assignment 93

Summary

Introduction

The Goldwater-Nichols Department of Defense (DoD) Reorganization Act of 1986 directed a broad range of organizational and functional changes to improve the military services' ability to carry out successful joint military operations. Title IV of the act contains the personnel provisions including management policies, promotion objectives, and education and experience for officers assigned to "joint" billets. However, the defense agencies and services have from the act's initial implementation raised numerous concerns about its provisions and procedures. Congress recognized these concerns and tasked DoD to revisit the implementation of Title IV of the Goldwater-Nichols legislation. The conferees of the 1993 National Defense Authorization Act reviewed the procedures, both statutory and regulatory, for designating a position as a joint duty assignment and concluded that "the time has come to reconsider the joint duty assignment list, particularly with respect to Defense Agencies."

In response to a request by the Director of Manpower and Personnel of the Joint Staff (JS/J-1), RAND examined the joint officer management that forms the basis of the response to the congressional directives. To effectively respond to Congress, the research approached the issue of joint officer management from both the demand and supply sides. The goal of the demand-side research was to recommend a procedure for identifying joint duty positions and to understand the implications of applying the procedure by generating several notional new Joint Duty Assignment Lists (JDALs); the goal of the supply-side research was to determine how large a JDAL the services could support. This report describes the results of the demand-side analysis.

Algorithm for Measuring the Joint Content of a Position

To begin our demand-side analysis, we created a way to measure the joint content of the various candidate positions. After using interviews and a literature review to identify some initial criteria for measuring joint content, we conducted five focus group sessions involving a total of forty people to help determine the final criteria—Joint Time, Joint Job Function, Non-Joint Job Function, and Number of Services. To determine scores for each of these criteria, researchers then analyzed the appropriate questions from a survey sent to the identified population of over 15,000 candidate joint duty billets (12,000 of the surveys were returned and processed).

Once the scores were determined, four algorithms were created that combined the criteria, starting with the simplest of relationships and progressively adding criteria to form more complex algorithms to determine if the added complexity affected the results. Based on this analysis, researchers determined that the joint content of billets can be adequately and sufficiently measured using a combination of Joint Time and Joint Function. Adding other variables results in a more complex relationship with little change in the resulting scores or rankings.

Applying the Joint Time/Joint Function algorithm enabled us to rank-order the positions based on the resulting scores. Several breakpoints in the ordered list are possible, although a degree of subjectivity is associated with any of them. Because of this subjectivity, the number of positions on a new JDAL should be determined in conjunction with the analysis on the number of joint positions that can be supported by the military services.

Implications of Applying the Joint Time/Joint Function Algorithm

To answer the specific questions of Congress, the algorithm was applied on a billet-by-billet basis to the survey responses received from the positions identified as potential JDAs, looking first at the implications of applying the Joint Time/Joint Function algorithm with the restrictions imposed by the law and by DoD policy. The impact of relaxing DoD policy of restricting O-3 positions from the JDAL and of changing the law to allow selected in-service positions to receive joint duty credit was next examined. Finally, we looked at the implications of applying a newly developed analytical approach for identifying critical billets.

Based on these analyses, we found that regardless of where the ordered list is "cut" to form a new JDAL, the following statements can be made:

- Virtually all the candidate billets have some joint content associated with them.
- Based purely on the joint content algorithm, no organization will have all its positions on a new JDAL (i.e., there will be no 100 percent organizations unless a policy decision dictates that all the applicable billets for a specific organization be on a new JDAL).

- Unlike under the current implementation of Goldwater-Nichols, defense agencies will not uniformly have 50 percent of their positions on a new JDAL. Some defense agencies will have a far lower percentage, while others will have a much higher percentage of their positions indicated as JDAs.
- Some O-3 and in-service positions have significant joint content. Including these positions on a new JDAL would require changing the law and current DoD policy.
- Using an objective, systematic approach to determine which positions are "critical joint billets" is preferred to the subjective approach organizations currently use. Based on reasonable criteria values, there are likely to be fewer, potentially many fewer, critical billets than the 1000 figure stated in Goldwater-Nichols.

Recommendations

Based on these results, we make the following recommendations:

- **Use the Joint Time/Joint Function algorithm to produce a joint content score for each billet**. Determine the size of a new JDAL (i.e., where to "cut" the ordered list) based on the number of joint positions the services can support (see the companion document, MR-593-JS). This will produce an initial minimum score for a billet to qualify for joint credit. Closely examine, using comparisons to similar billets and inputs from organizational commanders, the ten percent of the billets that lie above and below the minimum score to make final determinations of which positions are placed on a new JDAL.
- **Consider changing the DoD policy to allow O-3s to receive joint credit.** There are advantages and disadvantages associated with allowing O-3 positions on the JDAL. Further examine these advantages and disadvantages, especially in light of any proposed changes to the Goldwater-Nichols promotion comparisons.
- **Request changes to Goldwater-Nichols to:**
  — Allow in-service billets for grades of O-4 to O-6;
  — Employ a specific methodology for identifying critical billets.

Acknowledgments

We must first thank the more than 13,000 officers and civilians who took the time to answer a detailed survey to provide us with facts about their positions in diverse outside service organizations and with their opinions about joint officer management. Moreover, the authors are indebted to the staff of the Director for Manpower and Personnel (J-1) of the Joint Staff for their support, particularly Navy Captains Howard Nesbitt and Grant Fulkerson, Commanders David Logsdon and Cynthia Yarosh, and Major Diane Larson. Lieutenant Colonel John Hamlin of the Office of the Secretary of Defense contributed to our understanding of the Goldwater-Nichols legislation. Additionally, many officers in all of the military services helped us to understand how careers of officers are managed and how those careers are affected by joint duty assignments. In particular, we wish to acknowledge the officers from each service who served on the J-1 Study Group; they not only provided details on service personnel policies and practices but also data that allowed us to develop and validate models of joint assignments and promotion. We also appreciate the efforts of Steven Shupack of the Logistics Management Institute, for his expertise on issues involving the survey and the organization of the response data.

We are appreciative of the comments of Susan Hosek, Albert Robbert, Robert Howe, and Carolyn Libuser, who reviewed an earlier draft of the document and offered many helpful suggestions to clarify the presentation of the research methodology and findings.

We are aware that the views expressed in this report will not be supported by all service personnel managers. These are our views and do not represent the policy of the Department of Defense or the individual military departments.

Abbreviations and Acronyms

ACOM	Atlantic Command
CENTCOM	Central Command
CINC	Commander-in-Chief
COS	Critical Occupational Specialty
DFAS	Defense Finance and Accounting Service
DIA	Defense Intelligence Agency
DISA	Defense Information Systems Agency
DLA	Defense Logistics Agency
DMA	Defense Mapping Agency
DNA	Defense Nuclear Agency
DoD	Department of Defense
EUCOM	European Command
G/FOs	General/Flag Officers
GAO	Government Accounting Office
IG	Inspector General
JDA	Joint Duty Assignment
JDAL	Joint Duty Assignment List
JPME	Joint Professional Military Education
JS	Joint Staff
JSOs	Joint Specialty Officers
JSO noms	JSO nominees
NATO	North Atlantic Treaty Organization
NSA	National Security Agency
OSD	Office of the Secretary of Defense
PACOM	Pacific Command
SOCOM	Special Operations Command
SOUTHCOM	Southern Command
SPACECOM	Space Command
STRATCOM	Strategic Command
TRANSCOM	Transportation Command
USA	U.S. Army
USAF	U.S. Air Force
USMC	U.S. Marine Corps
USN	U.S. Navy
WHS	Washington Headquarters Service

1. Introduction

Background

The Goldwater-Nichols Department of Defense Reorganization Act of 1986

The Goldwater-Nichols Department of Defense (DoD) Reorganization Act of 1986 directed a broad range of organizational and functional changes to improve the ability of the military services to carry out successful joint military operations. Provisions in the act directed the Secretary of Defense to develop a definition of a Joint Duty Assignment (JDA) and to publish a Joint Duty Assignment List (JDAL). This list includes those positions at organizations, outside the individual services, that address issues involving multiple services or other nations where the assigned officer gains a "significant experience in joint matters."

Title IV of the act contains personnel-related provisions including management policies, promotion objectives, and education and experience requirements for officers assigned to "joint" billets. The major provisions of Title IV are contained in Chapter 38 of Title 10 of the United States Code.

The original implementation of Goldwater-Nichols, and the one that is used today, applied a broad-brush approach. Joint duty consideration was limited to pay grades of O-4 or higher. All such positions in some organizations (Office of the Secretary of Defense, the Joint Staff, and the unified commands) and half of the positions in each defense agency were placed on the JDAL. The law specifically prohibited positions in service organizations from receiving joint duty credit. This original implementation led to a list of approximately 8300 positions designated as JDAs.

Goldwater-Nichols Implementation Concerns

From the initial implementation of Goldwater-Nichols, concerns were raised by numerous organizations. The defense agencies expressed their concern that only half of their positions would qualify for joint assignments, whereas all the positions in other organizations were on the JDAL. The services felt that certain positions within the services (which we call "in-service" positions) had a joint content and should be considered for the JDAL. Finally, examples were noted of positions on the Joint Staff or the unified commands (where all positions above the grade of O-3 were granted joint duty credit) that had little or no joint content.

The services were also concerned about meeting the various constraints and promotion objectives specified by the law. They felt that it was difficult to qualify a sufficient number of officers to meet the "50 percent" rule of Goldwater-Nichols that required that at least half the positions on the JDAL *above the grade of O-3* be filled by Joint Specialty Officers (JSOs)[1] or officers nominated as JSOs (termed JSO noms). They also found it hard to manage their "quality" officers to ensure that sufficient numbers served in joint duty positions while adequately staffing positions in their own service with "quality" officers.

Some minor modifications were made during the ensuing years, such as a reduction in the tour length of joint duty assignments, but the basic stipulations of the law remain as originally written. The designation of positions that qualify for joint duty has also remained constant over the several years since the JDAL was first published.

Recent reductions in military personnel strength have exacerbated the problems faced by the services. The personnel demands of joint organizations have grown while the number of officers available to meet total demands has decreased. The services find it increasingly difficult to "share" their high-quality officers between the joint and service worlds.

Congressional Directive

Congress has recognized these concerns and has recently asked DoD to revisit the implementation of Goldwater-Nichols. The conferees of the 1993 National Defense Authorization Act reviewed the procedures, both statutory and regulatory, for designating a position as a joint duty assignment and concluded that "the time has come to reconsider the joint duty assignment list, particularly with respect to Defense Agencies." The conferees felt the 50 percent allocation had some unfortunate results. They believed it necessary to examine each position in the defense agencies to determine the correctness of its designation.

[1]Goldwater-Nichols established a new classification of officers. "Joint Specialty Officers" were to be "particularly trained in and oriented toward joint matters." Prerequisites to becoming a JSO include Joint Professional Military Education Phase II (JPME II) and a prior joint duty assignment. The majority of JSOs have completed both JPME II and a joint duty assignment, have been nominated by their service and selected by the Secretary of Defense with the advice of the Chairman of the Joint Chiefs of Staff. Officers who have reversed the order of their joint service and JPME, and officers who have served two joint tours, can also be selected as JSOs. These alternative paths are less frequent, and require waivers from the Secretary of Defense. Once selected as a JSO, the "tag" stays with an officer throughout his or her career.

Also, they raised the issue of reallocating joint duty assignment percentages among the agencies. The conferees regarded the exclusion of assignments within an officer's own Military Department as correct but were amenable to considering exceptions.

Section 932 of Public Law 102-484 (National Defense Authorization Act for Fiscal Year 1993) states: "The Secretary of Defense, after consultation with the Chairman of the Joint Chiefs of Staff, shall conduct a study of military officer positions that are designated as joint duty assignments pursuant to section 661 of Title 10, United States Code, and other provisions of the law." Two directives of Section 932 are to:

1. Assess the appropriateness of the current allocation of joint assignments and critical joint duty assignments with particular emphasis on the allocations to each defense agency;
2. Survey positions that provide military officers with a significant experience in joint matters but are now excluded from the joint duty designation under Section 661 of Title 10, United States Code, or other provisions of the law.

The conferees also identified a Government Accounting Office (GAO) study as containing a potential methodology for measuring the joint content of a position and suggested that the mandated study consider it.[2]

Objectives and Approach

The Director of Manpower and Personnel, the Joint Staff (JS/J-1), which is responsible for developing the response to the congressional directive, asked RAND to conduct research on joint officer management to assist in forming the basis for that response, including recommendations for a new implementation of the Goldwater-Nichols legislation that involves potential changes to the law and to OSD and service policies.

To effectively respond to the congressional directive, the research approached the issue of joint officer management from both the demand and supply sides. The goal of the demand-side research was to recommend a procedure for identifying joint duty positions and the approximate size and composition of a new JDAL; the goal of the supply-side research is to determine how large a JDAL the services could support.

---

[2]General Accounting Office, *Military Personnel: Designation of Joint Duty Assignments*, Report to Congressional Requesters, B-232940, February 1990.

Overall, the research met these objectives by using the following general approach:

1. Develop a preferred method (algorithm) to measure the joint content of a billet;
2. Survey all candidate billets through the use of a census;
3. Apply the preferred method to the billet census data to produce a list ordered on the basis of joint content;
4. Evaluate the implications of different notional lists;
5. Apply the supportability assessments for different-sized lists;
6. Provide recommendations.

This report focuses on the results of the demand-side analysis, which encompasses the first four tasks listed above. A companion document presents the results of the supply-side or supportability assessments reflected in Task 5 above.[3]

Identifying Criteria to Measure Joint Content

The first step in developing a method to measure a position's joint content was to identify the characteristics or attributes of a position that relate to its joint nature. An initial set of criteria arose from a review of the Goldwater-Nichols legislation and other important literature, including follow-on amendments to the law, congressional testimony on the law and its implementation, and reports and documents that examined various aspects of Goldwater-Nichols.

The initial criteria were substantiated and modified through numerous interviews with service personnel organizations, the Joint Staff, defense agencies, and congressional staffers who were originally involved with the drafting of the Goldwater-Nichols legislation. Group sessions were held with senior personnel from the services and various joint organizations to understand their perspectives on the relative importance of the candidate criteria for measuring the joint content of a position. The end result of this process was the identification of a set of criteria that would be used for further analysis.

Once an initial set of criteria was identified, a questionnaire was developed to capture the necessary data.

---

[3]See *How Many Can Be Joint? Supporting Joint Duty Assignments*, MR-593-JS, forthcoming.

Surveying Candidate Billets

Underlying both the demand and supply side of the analysis was a survey of the identified population of over 15,000 candidate joint duty billets. These positions, identified by the JS/J-1, included all the billets at the grade of O-3 or higher from the organizations currently represented on the JDAL, plus billets specifically nominated by the various military services. Therefore, the 15,000 candidate billets included all the positions currently on the JDAL plus other positions at the joint and service organizations that might be eligible for joint duty credit.

A survey instrument (see Appendix B) was tested first in a pilot survey sent to over 2000 billets in several joint organizations and defense agencies plus over 100 in-service billets. The questionnaire had three categories of questions. One set of questions gathered information on the person occupying the billet including grade, service, and skill. The second set of questions asked for details about the nature of duties and functions including time spent working with other services or nations. These questions provided the data used in the various methodologies. The third set of questions asked the respondents for their opinions on a variety of joint officer management issues.

This pilot survey served several purposes. First, it ensured that the instrument would capture the types of data necessary to produce values for the various criteria being developed to measure the joint content of a billet. More important, it ensured that the questions were worded and phrased in ways that were unambiguous to the respondents. To get "good" results, we needed "good" data for the algorithm. Since the census process would be time-consuming and costly, it was vital to attain quality data with a single survey process.

Second, the pilot survey data were needed to test the adequacy of the initial criteria and methodologies. Data were needed to test whether the scoring approaches could effectively measure the joint content of a position and would provide sufficient discrimination across all candidate positions.

Finally, the pilot survey helped provide the initial findings contained in the required interim report.[4] These findings included a preliminary response to the questions posed by Congress and a plan for completing the census and analyzing the data.

---

[4]The pilot survey process and initial findings were reported to the sponsor of this research in February 1994. That report formed the basis for the initial report to Congress entitled *Joint Duty Assignment Study (Interim Report)*, Under Secretary of Defense (Personnel and Readiness), June 1994.

Ultimately, the responses to the pilot survey helped determine which criteria to include in the algorithm and how to assign values to the criteria; it also helped reshape and reword several of the questions in the survey and helped provide a plan for the final analysis of the complete census data.

Over 15,000 surveys were mailed to the candidate billets during the first week of March 1994. When approximately 85 percent of the surveys were returned (July 1994), a data set was prepared for analysis. An overview of the survey responses by organizational grouping is shown in Table 1.1.

The warfighting commanders-in-chief (CINCs) include the United States Atlantic Command (ACOM), Pacific Command (PACOM), European Command (EUCOM), Central Command (CENTCOM), and Southern Command (SOUTHCOM). The supporting CINCs include the United States Transportation Command (TRANSCOM), Special Operations Command (SOCOM), Strategic Command (STRATCOM), and Space Command (SPACECOM). The WHS/OSD category includes positions in the various organizations of the Office of the Secretary of Defense (OSD) and in the Washington Headquarters Service (WHS). The in-service category includes the billets within their own organizations nominated by the Army, Navy, Air Force, and Marine Corps. Finally, the All others category includes organizations not captured in the other groupings and represents primarily positions with NATO-oriented organizations.

Table 1.1

Survey Responses

Organization	Surveys Sent	Percent Returned	Usable Surveys	Current JDAs in Usable Surveys
Joint Staff	795	97	741	739
Defense agencies	4,364	90	3,466	1,291
Warfighting CINCs	3,191	87	2,608	2,193[a]
Supporting CINCs	2,158	97	2,002	1,468
WHS/OSD[b]	741	80	565	414
In-service	1,584	69	839	113[c]
All others	2,395	73	1,806	962
Total	**15,228**	**85**	**12,027**	**7,180**

NOTE: Responses received as of 7/21/94.

[a]The difference between the number of usable surveys and the current number of JDAs reflects O-3 positions.

[b]Washington Headquarters Service.

[c]Dual-hatted or cross-service positions such as an Air Force officer assigned to the Military Sealift Command. These are termed in-service because they are positions in service (versus joint) organizations.

Not all of the surveys received were processed. Each survey was checked for numerical accuracy. When mistakes were discovered, they were corrected if the mistake was minor in nature or if researchers could infer from the responses the respondent's intent. Most of the mistakes were correctable; however, approximately 700 of the surveys were determined to be unusable and were returned to the respondents for corrections. Slightly over 12,000 surveys were available for analysis.

Responses from initial and subsequent mailings continue to come in. At the time of this writing, an additional 1800 surveys were available at the processing organization. However, nine months from the initial mailing, approximately 1500 surveys were still outstanding. Although we will ultimately be able to process responses from some 90 percent of the candidate billets, there will be billets we will not be able to evaluate. The recommendations of this research are not affected by the outstanding surveys, but implementation of a new joint duty assignment procedure may require a complete census of all candidate positions.

Organization of the Report

Section 2 focuses on the demand analysis, describing the initial research to identify a set of criteria for measuring the joint content of a position, as well as the research approach that led to a final set of criteria and the preferred methodology for measuring the joint content of a position. Section 3 discusses the application of the results of the demand analysis to the survey data, comparing the composition of two potential new JDALs to the current JDAL by organization, service, grade, and skill. It provides these comparisons both for the current law and DoD policy and if current law and/or policy were changed. The section also summarizes a methodology for identifying critical billets and shows the implications of applying such a methodology. Section 4 summarizes conclusions from the demand-side analysis and presents recommendations.

Several appendices present details on specific aspects of the research. Appendix A provides an overview of the personnel provisions of the Goldwater-Nichols legislation. Appendix B contains a copy of the survey instrument sent to all candidate billets. Appendix C presents the results of group sessions that were designed to solicit the views on different methodologies and criteria from senior decisionmakers. Appendix D provides results from a set of opinion questions included in the survey instrument.

2. Conducting the Demand-Side Analysis

To evaluate the adequacy of the current DoD implementation of the Goldwater-Nichols legislation, an analytical approach was needed to measure the joint content of the various candidate positions. Applying the measurement methodology to the data collected from the survey of all the positions would enable a list to be produced ordered from high joint content to low joint content. This rank-ordered list would then form the basis for the response to the questions raised by Congress and for building a new JDAL.

In this section, we discuss how we determined the attributes or characteristics of a position that are related to joint matters and the joint content of a position; combined these attributes in one or more analytical ways (i.e., an algorithm) to produce a joint "score" for a position; applied the algorithm(s) to the census data to produce a list ordered from "most joint" to "least joint;" and used statistical procedures to identify groups with similar joint content and develop notional JDALs based on combinations of these groups.

Determining Factors for Measuring Joint Content

Preliminary Reviews

The legal code that implemented Goldwater-Nichols[1] applied the term "joint duty assignment" to assignments in which the officer gains significant experience in **joint matters**. It defined joint matters as:

> matters relating to the integrated employment of land, sea, and air forces, including matters relating to (1) national military strategy; (2) strategic planning and contingency planning; and (3) command and control of combat operations under unified command.

The law also required the Secretary of Defense to provide a definition of joint duty assignment. The Department of Defense subsequently defined a **joint duty assignment** as:

> an assignment to a designated position in a multi-service or multi-national command or activity that is involved in the integrated employment *or*

[1]Section 668(a), Chapter 38, Title 10, United States Code (as amended through December 31, 1992), April 1993, U.S. Government Printing Office, Washington, DC.

> *support* [emphasis added] of the land, sea, and air forces of at least two of the three Military Departments. Such involvement includes, but is not limited to, matters relating to national military strategy, joint doctrine and planning, strategic planning, contingency planning, and command and control of combat operations under a unified command.[2]

The DoD definition of a joint duty assignment was similar to the definition of joint matters contained in Goldwater-Nichols, with two important extensions. First, DoD expanded the notion of "jointness" to include not only the **employment** but also the **support** of joint operations. Second, it broadened the types of activities included in joint matters by specifically adding joint doctrine and joint policy and by using the term "but is not limited to" to leave open the possibility of other types of job functions.

The legal definition of joint matters and the DoD definition of joint duty assignment contain two important notions for identifying attributes or characteristics related to the joint content of a position. First, one interpretation of the term "significant experience" suggests a temporal dimension or the amount of time spent on joint matters. Second, by listing specific types of activities, both DoD and Goldwater-Nichols imply that joint content is related to what a person does in his job, that is, to a position's functions and duties.

In addition to examining the law and the DoD definitions, we reviewed other primary literature, including follow-on amendments to the law, congressional testimony on the law and its implementation, and various reports and documents that examined various aspects of Goldwater-Nichols. In conjunction with these literature reviews, we interviewed a wide range of people from various organizations, both within the defense establishment and on congressional staffs, seeking to understand their impressions of the intent of the law, how the law should be implemented, what constitutes joint matters, and how to measure the joint content of a position. The primary objective of these literature reviews, interviews, and discussions was to identify a set of characteristics useful for measuring the joint content of a billet.

The GAO study,[3] specifically referred to in the congressional tasking, was an important source of information during the initial stages of the research. The GAO study team developed a system to place positions into one of six categories. These categories distinguished between joint versus single service activities and

---

[2]Joint Chiefs of Staff, *Joint Officer Management*, JCS Administrative Publication 1.2, Washington, DC, June 1989.

[3]General Accounting Office, *Military Personnel: Designation of Joint Duty Assignments*, Report to Congressional Requesters, B-232940, February 1990.

between the operational content of the position's duties and responsibilities.[4] The last two categories—containing officers assigned to joint organizations but doing work primarily involving his or her own service—were considered to be nonjoint positions by GAO.

GAO conducted desk-side interviews with approximately 400 officers assigned to various joint organizations and defense agencies. Based on the data collected during these interviews, officers were placed into one of the six categories. Although the report provided no specific recommendations, the GAO analysts felt that many of the defense agency positions that were not designated as joint duty assignments did provide a joint operational experience and that some of the positions from the joint organizations had little or no joint content. They also expressed the concerns of DoD officials and some of the negative aspects surrounding an operationally focused Joint Duty Assignment List.

Several important insights came from the GAO study. First, defining the duties and responsibilities of a position was important along with distinguishing between single service and multi-service job functions. Second, the basic interview methodology used by GAO had to be modified to capture the needed data from the thousands of candidate positions.

Identification of Initial Criteria

Based on the initial interviews and literature review, we identified five attributes or characteristics of a position that could potentially prove useful for measuring the joint content of a position. These five criteria[5] were:

1. **Joint Time**—the proportion of a billet's time spent on matters involving other services or other nations.
2. **Job Function**—what people do in their job, including the areas they work in and the duties they perform.
3. **Number of Services**—the number of services a person interacts with in performing their job function.

---

[4]The six GAO categories were (1) joint operational, (2) joint operational (related), (3) joint non-operational, (4) joint technical and administrative, (5) single service operational, and (6) single service.

[5]We will use the more technical term "criteria" for the remainder of the report to signify attributes or characteristics of a position.

4. **Organizational Level**—the position of a billet within an organization's hierarchy and the position of an organization within the overall defense hierarchy.
5. **Grade**—the military grade or rank of the billet.

Conducting Focus Group Sessions

To help determine the final criteria for analysis, we conducted five group sessions involving over forty people. The five sessions included: (1) representatives from the J-1 directorates of various Unified Commands and defense agencies; (2) the general/flag officers (G/FOs) from each service that comprise the J-1's Executive Council for the report to Congress; (3) senior officers from the various directorates of the Joint Staff; (4) representatives from each of the services' personnel planning organizations; and (5) representatives from each of the defense agencies.

At each session, the participants were led through a computer-assisted structured interview designed to gather their opinions on various weights and values to assign to the initial criteria. Their views on the relative importance of each of the initial criteria for measuring the joint content of a billet were recorded and transformed into numerical weights. The resulting weights form the coefficients for the criteria in the multi-criteria scoring methodology. The average weights from the various sessions are shown in Table 2.1.[6]

As Table 2.1 shows, Joint Time and Job Function were the two criteria that were most important for measuring the joint content of a billet. Together, they had been assigned almost 70 percent of the total weight and their individual weights were approximately equal.

Table 2.1

Average Criteria Weights from Group Sessions

Criteria	Average Weight
Joint Time	0.32
Job Function	0.36
Number of Services	0.15
Organizational Context	0.12
Military Grade	0.05

[6]Saaty's Analytic Hierarchy Process was used to derive the weights. This methodology is described in T. L. Saaty, *The Analytic Hierarchy Process*, McGraw-Hill, New York, 1980. Detailed results from the group sessions are contained in Appendix C.

The Number of Services and the Organizational Context criteria were assigned about equal weights, although their weights were less than half the weight for Joint Time or Job Function. Finally, the weight for Military Grade was very low.

Ten functional duties and twenty-nine subject matter areas were identified during the pilot survey. These duties and areas together form a description of a job's function (one of the initial criteria). A second software package elicited the participants' opinions of the relative value of each of the ten duties and of each of the twenty-nine subject areas. The average values for the functional duties and the subject areas are displayed in Tables 2.2 and 2.3, respectively.

One other issue was explored during some of the group sessions. The GAO study made a distinction between matters involving an officer's own service and matters involving multiple services. Also, interviews, discussions, and logical arguments suggested that the joint content of a billet should be based on the joint aspects of a position. Therefore, the participants in the last two groups (14 of the 41 participants) were asked for their views of the relative importance of the joint (multiple service) versus nonjoint (officer's own service or organization) aspects of a job's functions. On average, the group participants placed twice the weight on joint function compared to nonjoint function.

Determining Final Criteria for Analysis

Based on all the analyses, we selected the following four criteria:

1. **Joint Time**—the proportion of a billet's time spent on matters involving other services or other nations.

Table 2.2

Average Values for Functional Duties

Functional Duty	Average Value
Command/control of combat/combat support	10
Conduct military operations	9
Develop, staff, or implement plans	8
Support military operations	7
Command/control of noncombat units	6
Develop, staff, assess requirements	6
Develop, staff, assess doctrine	5
Develop, staff, assess policies	5
Develop, assess program/budget submissions	3
Provide administrative or technical support	2

NOTE: These functional duties correspond to the options listed for question 13 of the survey (see Appendix B).

Table 2.3

Average Values for Subject Areas

Subject Area	Average Value
National Military Strategy	10.0
Strategic Matters	9.0
Tactical Matters	8.0
Special Operations	8.0
Logistics	8.0
Operations Other Than War	7.5
Force Development	7.5
Intelligence	7.5
Communications	7.0
Mobilization	6.5
Training (other than exercises)	5.0
Nuclear, Chemical, Biological	5.0
Politico-Military or Attaché Matters	4.5
Acquisition/R&D	4.5
Mapping, Charting, Geodesy	4.0
Education and Professional Development	4.0
Manpower and Personnel	4.0
Medical/Health Services	3.5
Automatic Data Processing	3.5
Engineering	3.5
Scientific Matters	3.5
Resource/Financial Management	3.0
Contracting/Contract Management	2.5
Law Enforcement	2.0
Public Affairs	2.0
Inspector General	1.5
General Administration	1.5
Legislative Affairs	1.5
Legal Affairs	1.5

NOTE: These subject areas correspond to the options listed for question 14 of the survey (see Appendix B).

2. **Joint Job Function**—what people do in their job, including the areas they work in and the duties they perform, when working on matters involving multiple services or other nations.
3. **Nonjoint Job Function**—what people do in their job, including the areas they work in and the duties they perform, when working on matters involving their own service or organization.
4. **Number of Services**—the number of services a person interacts with in performing their job function.

In the process of selection, Organizational Context and Grade were eliminated. In addition to having the lowest weight of the initial criteria, we felt it would be difficult and highly subjective to assign values to these two criteria. Responses to the survey questions had to yield values for the criteria in a logical and objective way, such as for the Joint Time variable. More joint time results in a higher score than less joint time, and twice the amount of joint time should result in twice the score. The values from the group sessions for functional duties and responsibilities provided a method to assign scores to the Joint and Nonjoint Function criteria.

However, this is not true for Grade and Organizational Context. One may reason that the higher the grade associated with a position, the higher the value for that criterion. But this relationship is not obvious if the objective is to measure the joint content of a position. Also, such an approach would bias a new JDAL toward the higher grades, potentially causing problems for the services in supporting the new list. Finally, the experience an officer gains from a joint assignment may be most valuable during the early stages of a career when the joint experience can help shape attitudes, values, beliefs, and perspectives. Senior officers may actually draw less benefit from an initial joint tour than junior officers.

A similar problem exists for the Organizational Context criterion. How does one attach a value to different levels within an organization's hierarchy, or to different organizations within the defense establishment?

Combining Criteria to Produce a Joint Score for a Billet

In this subsection, we show how we calculated the scores for each of the selected criteria chosen, how we developed a multi-attribute methodology to combine criteria into algorithms, and how we selected a preferred algorithm.

Calculating Scores for the Selected Criteria

The scores for each of the selected criteria were determined by analyzing the appropriate questions in the survey instrument (see Appendix B). The scores were calculated on a zero to ten basis.

Number of Services. Question 18 of the survey instrument asked the respondents to indicate "the military Services you interact with in the performance of your primary duties and responsibilities." The distribution of the responses for all the surveys processed is shown in Figure 2.1.

Figure 2.1 shows the majority of respondents indicated they interacted with all four military services.

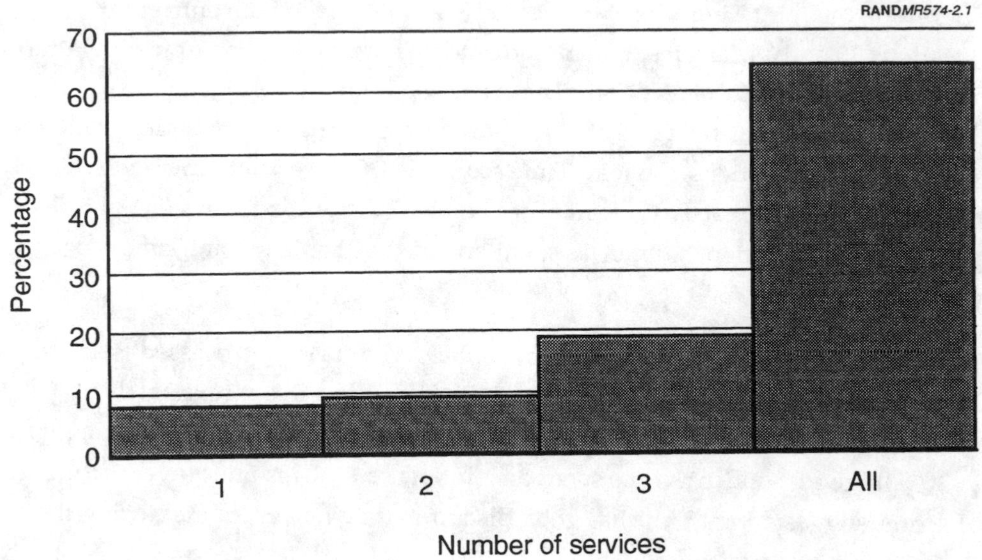

Figure 2.1—Distribution of Number of Services Score

Joint Time. Question 13[7] of the survey instrument asks respondents to report the time they spend in various activities along two dimensions. First, they report the average proportion of their time they spend in each of the ten functional duties (i.e., those listed in Table 2.2). For each functional duty where there is a time entry, they spread the total time to matters involving their own service or organization, matters involving multiple services, and matters involving other nations. We consider the first category to be nonjoint time and the last two categories to be joint time.

Question 14 is similar. It asks each respondent to first report the proportion of their time they spend in each of the twenty-nine subject areas (i.e., those listed in Table 2.3) and then to spread the time to matters involving their own service or organization, multiple services, and other nations. Again, we consider the first category to be time spent on nonjoint activities and the last two to be time spent on joint activities.

The score for the Joint Time variable was based on the sum of the entries for the multiple services and other nations categories in questions 13 and 14 in the survey. Theoretically, the sum of the joint time for question 13 should equal the sum of the joint time for question 14. However, this was not always the case.[8]

---

[7]See Appendix B for a copy of the survey instrument.

[8]When the time entries for questions 13 and 14 did not sum to 100 percent, one of two actions was taken. If the sum of the entries was between 80 percent and 120 percent, the entries were

Therefore, the Joint Time score was based on an average of both entries for questions 13 and 14. If a respondent indicated he or she spent no time on matters involving multiple services or other nations,[9] the Joint Time score was zero. If the respondent spent 100 percent of his or her time on matters involving multiple services or other nations, the Joint Time score was 10. The Joint Time score was measured proportionately for joint times between the two extremes (i.e., if 50 percent of a respondent's time was spent on joint matters, the Joint Time score was 5).

The distribution of the Joint Time score for all of the surveys processed is shown in Figure 2.2. The figure shows that the Joint Time score is approximately uniformly distributed between the scores of 1 and 9 with a peak at a score equal to 10 (all the respondent's time spent on joint matters). This uniform distribution of scores suggests Joint Time has good discriminating power for measuring the joint content of a position.

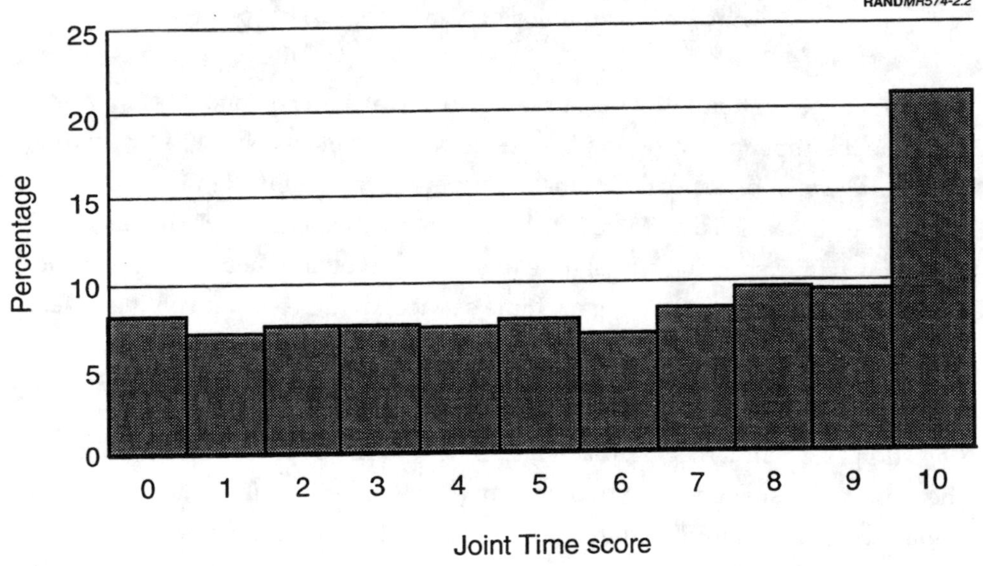

Figure 2.2—Distribution of Joint Time Score

---

adjusted using a normalization procedure. For example, if the sum of the time entries was 80 percent, each entry was multiplied by 1.25 (100 divided by 80). If the time entries totaled less than 80 percent or more than 120 percent, the individual responses were checked manually. If the source of the error could be inferred from the responses, the entries were corrected. If no inferences could be made, the survey was designated as unusable and returned to the respondent for corrections.

One other check was made on the responses to questions 13 and 14. In addition to the ten functional duties and twenty-nine subject areas, an additional entry was provided for "other" duty or area that was not specifically listed among the various options for the respondent to write in. When entries were made in this "other" category, the response was manually checked. Based on the response, the time entered under "other" was placed into one of the defined duties or areas.

[9]Approximately 770 surveys indicated no joint time.

Joint and Nonjoint Function. The calculations for the Joint and Nonjoint Function scores were slightly more complex. One concern was to keep the Joint Function score independent of the Joint Time score to avoid correlation of the two criteria. Therefore, the Joint Function (and Nonjoint Function) score was calculated independent of how much time was spent on joint matters (or nonjoint matters).[10]

Because Joint Time and Joint Function are independent of each other, attention must be paid to the relative weights assigned to these two variables. A position can receive a high Joint Function score when actually little time is spent on joint matters. If too high a weight is placed on Joint Function relative to Joint Time, a high score will result for a position that in reality is concerned primarily with its own service or organization.

Each of the ten functional duties in question 13 and the twenty-nine subject areas in question 14 had an assigned value (shown in Tables 2.2 and 2.3) based on the results of the group sessions. If respondents spent all their joint time (regardless of how much time) in one duty or one area, they received the corresponding duty score or area score. If they spent their joint time in two or more functional duties or subject areas, the scores were weighted proportionately based on the fraction of their joint time in each duty or area. As an example, if respondents said they spent 50 percent of their joint time (independent of how much time in total) in the Special Operations area (value of 8.0) and 50 percent of their joint time in the Manpower and Personnel area (value of 4.0), they received a joint area score of 6.0 (50 percent of the 8.0 plus 50 percent of the 4.0). Similar rules were used for the calculation of the joint duty score.

The resulting score for Joint Function was an average of the joint duty score from question 13 and the joint area score from question 14. The Nonjoint Function score was calculated in a similar way based on the time spent on matters involving a respondent's own service or organization.

The distribution of the Joint Function and Nonjoint Function scores for all the surveys processed are shown in Figures 2.3 and 2.4, respectively. These figures show the majority of the scores are in the 3 to 7 range.

---

[10]Statistical correlation analysis found the resulting Joint Time and Joint Function scores to be independent.

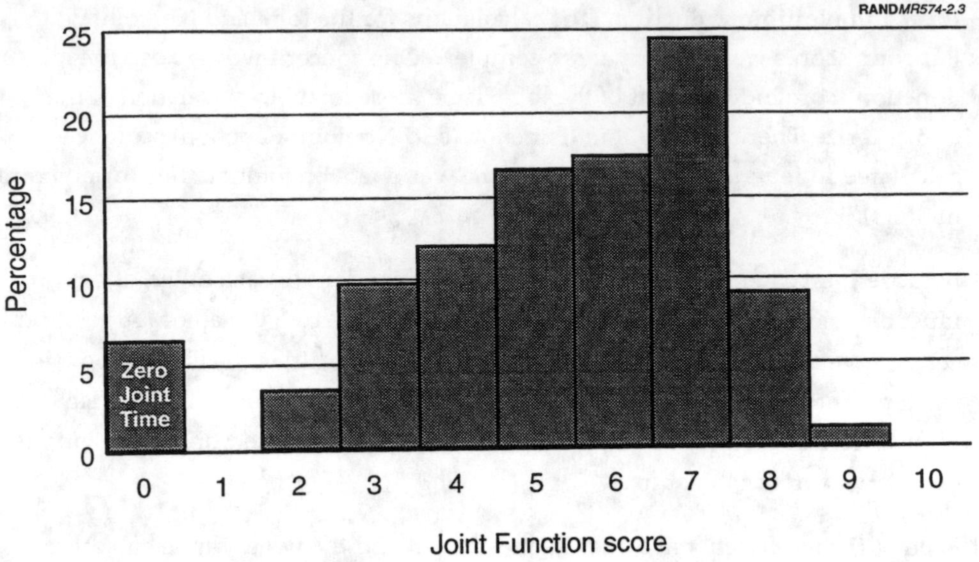

Figure 2.3—Distribution of Joint Function Score

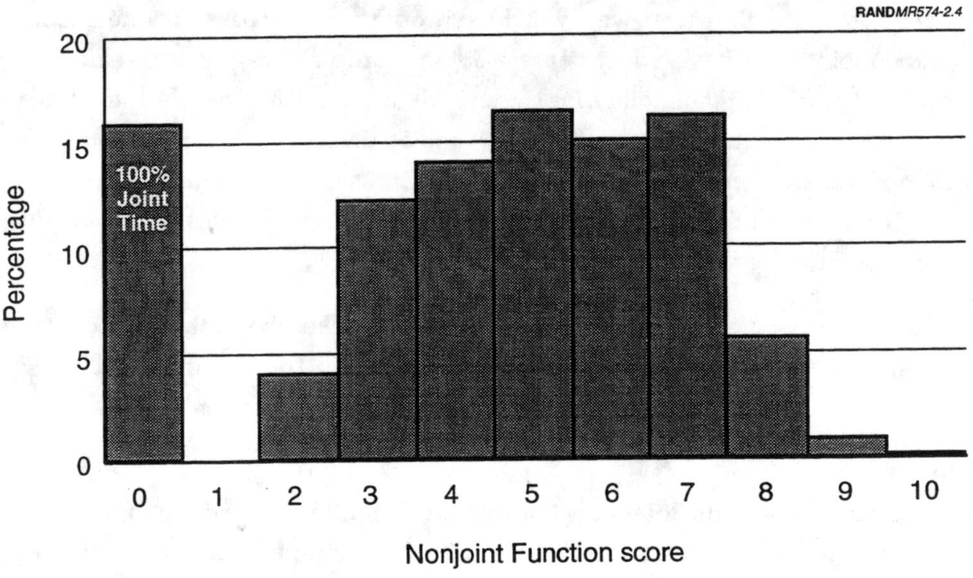

Figure 2.4—Distribution of Nonjoint Function Score

Developing Algorithms Combining Scored Criteria

Our ultimate objective was to produce an algorithm using these scored criteria or a subset of the criteria that was simple yet effective. We wanted to avoid an "overspecified" algorithm, or one that included more criteria (i.e., more complex) than necessary to adequately measure joint content.

We adopted an analysis procedure, similar to a stepwise regression analysis, that started with the simplest of relationships and progressively added criteria to form more complex algorithms. At each step, we compared the results of the algorithms in an attempt to understand if the added complexity affected the results.

We identified the following four algorithms for measuring a position's joint content:

- Algorithm 1: Score = JT
- Algorithm 2: Score = 50% JT + 50% JF
- Algorithm 3: Score = 40% JT + 40% JF + 20% #Svcs
- Algorithm 4: Score = 45% JT + 30% JF + 15% NJF + 10% #Svcs

where JT = Joint Time

JF = Joint Job Function

#Svcs = Number of Services

NJF = Nonjoint Job Function.

Comparing Results Across the Various Algorithms

Each algorithm produced a score for each of the more than 12,000 surveys processed. Figure 2.5 shows the results for each of the four algorithms described previously plus the scores based solely on Joint Function. The Y-axis in the graph is the joint score indexed from zero to one hundred. The X-axis corresponds to the number of surveys that had a given score or higher. For example, all the curves show that approximately 6000 positions had joint index scores of 60 or higher.

Algorithm 1 (score based just on Joint Time) is approximately linear, reflecting the uniform distribution shown in Figure 2.1. The score of 100 for the first 2000 positions reflects officers that spend all their time on joint matters. The remaining algorithms, plus the Joint Function score, produce a different, similarly S-shaped curve compared to algorithm 1. This suggests that there is a marked difference in the results when Joint Function is added to Joint Time, but adding other variables to algorithm 2 has little or no effect on the distribution of joint scores.

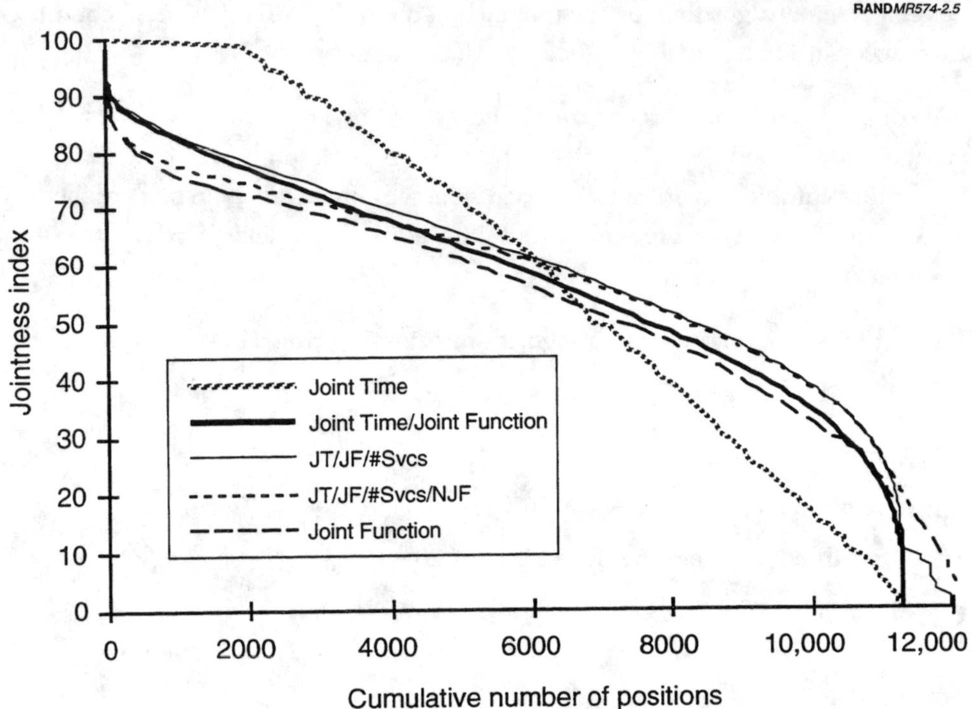

Figure 2.5—Results of Algorithm Analysis

One other method was used to compare the four algorithms. Three different notional-sized lists were extracted from the rank-ordered lists produced by the four algorithms. That is, we assumed a new JDAL would be approximately the same size as the current JDAL and "cut" the list at that point (approximately 7000 positions). We also assumed the list would be approximately 25 percent smaller (a "cut" at 5000 positions) and approximately 25 percent larger (a "cut" at 9000 positions). Thus, for each of the four algorithms we had three "new" JDALs for analysis.

For each of the new lists (i.e., for each "cut point"), we matched the billets on the list across the four algorithms. In each case, there was a significant difference in the content of a "new" JDAL when comparing algorithm 1 to algorithm 2. However, the results from algorithm 3 and algorithm 4 were virtually identical to the results from algorithm 2.

Selecting a Preferred Algorithm

Comparisons across the four algorithms suggest that a relationship including Joint Time and Joint Function is effective for measuring the joint content of a position and that adding other criteria to this basic relationship does not materially change the resulting rank order of the positions. Therefore, we believe algorithm 2 is the appropriate methodology for ranking billets based on their joint content.

In addition to the analytical rationale for selecting algorithm 2, the choice is logically appealing. As described previously, the Number of Services variable is heavily skewed, suggesting it has little discriminating power for comparisons across the various positions. Also, there was a question of whether an algorithm designed to measure the joint content of a billet should have criteria that were related to the nonjoint aspects of a position. *Including only Joint Time and Joint Function in the algorithm keeps the methodology purely in the joint world.* Finally, the two criteria in algorithm 2 are the ones that are consistent with the legal and DoD definitions of joint matters and joint duty assignment and with the methodology developed in the earlier GAO study.

Potential Variation of Algorithm 2. Algorithm 2 is based on a simple additive combination of the Joint Time and Joint Function scores.[11] There are other ways that the Joint Time and Joint Function criteria could be combined to produce a rank-ordered list. For example, a multiplicative form would produce a joint score that is the product of the Joint Time and Joint Function scores. Or the additive and multiplicative forms could be combined to produce a joint score that is based on the addition of three component scores—Joint Time, Joint Function, and the product of the two.

However, using a different functional combination of Joint Time and Joint Function affects only the ranking of the billets around the "cut point." That is, once a size is determined for a new JDAL, different algorithms using the same criteria will impact only the bottom (approximately) ten percent of the list. But other subjectivities in the overall approach, including the subjectivity of the criteria weights, values for different functional duties and subject areas, and the data provided by the respondents, also affect this lower portion of a new JDAL.

One problem with the additive form of the algorithm is that a mid-range score can result for a position that scores very high in one criterion but very low in the other. For example, a position with a Joint Time score of 9 and a Joint Function score of 3 would have an overall joint score of 6. This score would rank the billet

[11]We examined several variations of the different algorithms including changing the values of the coefficients, including all the initial criteria with the weights suggested from the group sessions, and modifying the values for the different functional duties and subject matter areas. The results of these sensitivity analyses consistently suggested that changes to the basic Joint Time/Joint Function algorithm had minimal impact on the rank order of the positions.

ahead of a position with a 5.5 score for both Joint Time and Joint Function. This result is an artifact of using the additive form. Using other forms such as the multiplicative does not completely resolve this. Moreover, the additive form is easy to calculate and understand, and one can readily see the individual contribution of each criterion.

Our analysis suggests that Joint Time and Joint Function are the proper criteria for measuring the joint content of a position. We use a simple additive form of these two criteria. Other functional forms could be used, and would result in a slight difference in the positions that score above a particular "cut point."

Cautions in Using Any Algorithm. The multi-criteria algorithm used to score and rank-order the candidate positions based on joint content is an analytical approach that uses various numerical factors and data. Although the methodology is numerical and analytical in nature, it is not purely objective. There are a number of subjective inputs and opinions that underlie whatever algorithm is adopted.

The three primary issues we addressed in the development of the algorithm were which criteria to use, how much relative weight to place on each criterion, and how to generate scores for the various criteria. In terms of the appropriate criteria, we based our choice on a review of the literature, interviews with officials, results from group sessions, and analysis of the data. Our research suggested that Joint Time and Joint Function are the two primary criteria. Other criteria could be included in the algorithm, but they would change the resulting scores and rankings very little while creating additional problems with generating criteria scores.

Our choice of weights for the two criteria and the values used to generate the score for the Joint Function criterion are based solely on averages of individual responses in the group sessions. Although there was typically a consensus on the relative ordering of criteria from most to least important, there was a large degree of variability in the specific weights for some of the measures. Plus, the weights and values are based on the subjective inputs of the participants and not on objective analytical analysis.

There is also the issue of the data from the survey instruments. We asked respondents to spread their time in several dimensions—to various functional duties, to a range of subject areas, and to matters involving multiple services, other nations, or their own service or organization. There is a degree of subjectivity in the responses and, therefore, in the data we use to generate joint scores. In most cases, the person filling the position provided the data. However, in approximately 20 percent of the cases, the position was not occupied at the time of the survey. In those situations, a supervisor or someone else responded to the survey questions.

In addition to some degree of subjectivity in the responses, there is the potential that the question may have been misunderstood by the respondent. Although we tested the various questions with pretests and a pilot survey, some respondents may have found some questions ambiguous.

Because of the various sources of subjectivity, the results of the algorithm should not be viewed as "the answer." Rather, the scores and rankings produced by the Joint Time/Joint Function algorithm are a starting point for determining a new JDAL. The data and the algorithm can indicate those positions that should be on, or not be on, a JDAL. There will be, however, a number of positions around the "cut line" that will require closer examination.

The disposition of those billets that just fall on, or off, a new JDAL should be determined by comparison with like positions within the same organization or similar billets at other organizations. There should be consistency in the determination of a new JDAL, a consistency that will not come from the algorithmic process alone. The commander of an organization should have input regarding which of his organization's positions should be granted joint duty credit. Although the analytical process and the precision implied by the numbers is appealing, the results must be tempered by sound judgment.

Determining the Potential Size of a New JDAL

The selection of algorithm 2 results only in a procedure for scoring and ranking the various positions. A second issue is where to "cut" the resulting list, or what minimum score identifies a "significant joint experience" and, therefore, results in a position receiving joint duty credit. This issue will help determine the size of a new JDAL.

Cluster Analysis

One method for determining the size of a new JDAL was suggested in the interim report to Congress:[12] a statistical procedure termed cluster analysis. Cluster analysis is a term applied to a range of techniques for determining

[12]See *Joint Duty Assignment Study (Interim Report)*, Under Secretary of Defense (Personnel and Readiness), June 1994.

"natural groups" or clusters in sets of data. The objectives, and limitations, of cluster analysis can be stated as:

> The objective is to group either the data units or the variables into clusters such that the elements within a cluster have a high degree of *natural association* among themselves while the clusters are *relatively distinct* from one another. The approach to the problem and the results achieved depend principally on how the investigator chooses to give operational meaning to the phrases *natural association* and *relatively distinct.*[13]

Other Statistical Techniques

Because of the subjectivity in the application of cluster analysis techniques, we also considered other techniques for determining potential breakpoints in the rank-order list.

We first applied the cluster analysis procedure using various numbers of clusters (from two to ten).[14] We then matched the resulting clusters to other statistical techniques. One such technique was to use the median score (the score where half of the positions had higher scores and the other half had lower scores). The median score of 5.8 corresponded closely to the boundary between the second and third cluster in a five-cluster grouping.

We also used the lower inflection point in the curve for algorithm 2 shown in Figure 2.5. This inflection point, which occurs at a score of approximately 4.0, corresponds to the boundary between the third and fourth cluster of a five-cluster grouping.

Applying the Techniques

Figure 2.6 shows the distribution of joint scores from algorithm 2 with the two potential breakpoints indicated.

The Y-axis in Figure 2.6 displays the number of positions with the specific scores shown on the X-axis. For example, there are approximately 130 positions that have a score of 5.8. The breakpoint of 5.8 corresponds to the median score and includes the first two groups of five clusters. The breakpoint of 4.0 corresponds

---

[13]Michael R. Anderberg, *Cluster Analysis for Applications*, Academic Press, San Diego, Calif., 1973.

[14]The Logistics Management Institute (LMI) performed the cluster analysis using a K-means cluster analysis heuristic with our algorithm 2 scores.

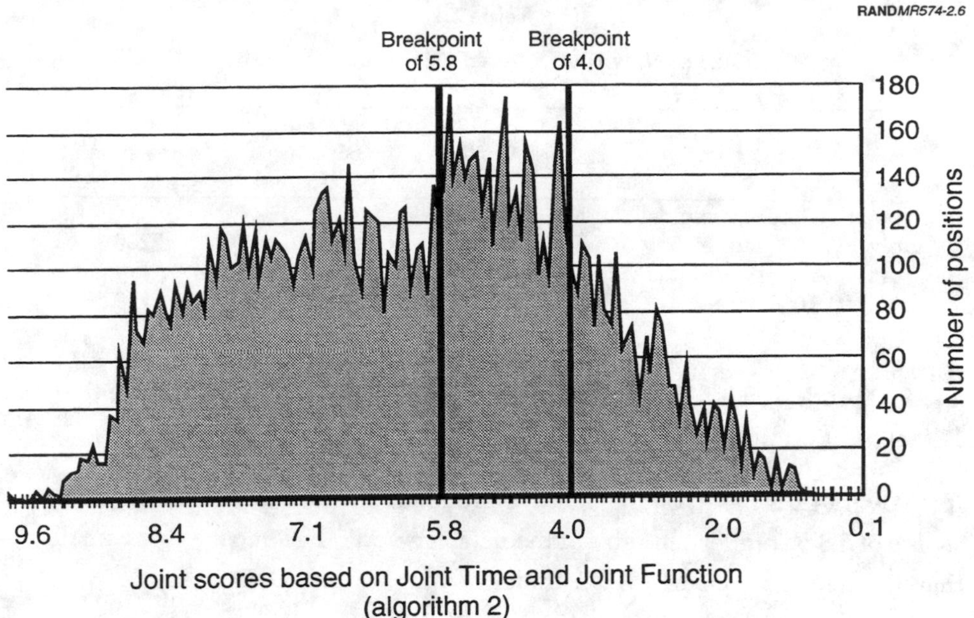

Figure 2.6—Distribution of Joint Scores from Algorithm 2

to the inflection point in the algorithm 2 curve of Figure 2.5 and includes the first three clusters.

Although these two potential breakpoints have a theoretical basis, they are still subjective. The billets to the right of each breakpoint (i.e., those with lower scores) still have joint content. In the case of the group 1 and 2 breakpoint, many of the scores to the right have fairly high Joint Time and/or Joint Function scores. Because of this concern, it is important that the size of a new JDAL be determined in conjunction with analysis of the ability of the services to support joint duty assignments. This "supportability" analysis is the topic of MR-593-JS, *How Many Can Be Joint? Supporting Joint Duty Assignments.*

Determining a Potential New JDAL

Table 2.4 compares the size of the new JDALs based on the two breakpoints with the size of the current JDAL for both the 12,000 surveys processed and for an extrapolation to the full 15,000 candidate population. The table shows the size of the JDAL based on the current law restricting in-service billets from the JDAL and the current DoD policy restricting O-3 grades from receiving joint duty credit—4900 positions (groups 1–2) and 7200 positions (groups 1–3) for 12,000,

Table 2.4

Size of New JDALs Based on Scoring Algorithm

List	Current JDAL	New JDAL Based on Groups 1–2	New JDAL Based on Groups 1–3
Total JDAL for current law and policy (12,000 surveys)	7200	4900	7200
Total JDAL for current law and policy (15,000 surveys)	9100	5900	8700

and 9100 and 5900 for 15,000.[15] In the remainder of the analysis, we use the 12,000 position figures.

If a new JDAL is based on the first two groups in the rank-ordered list (joint scores of 5.8 or higher), the size of the new list would be almost a third smaller than the size of the current JDAL under current law and DoD policy.

If a new JDAL is based on the first three groups (joint scores of 4.0 or higher), the size of the new list would be slightly smaller than the size of the current JDAL. The next section describes the implications by organization, service, grade, and skill of the two potential "new" JDALs shown in Table 2.4.

---

[15]For each organization, we calculated the percentage of the billets we processed that were in groups 1, 2, and 3. We used these percentages to estimate the number of unprocessed billets at each organization that might have been in the three groups. The exception to this general rule was for in-service billets, where we assumed that the positions that did not return a survey would not be granted joint credit.

3. Implications of Applying the Joint Time/Joint Function Algorithm

Determining an adequate methodology for measuring the joint content of a billet is only the first step in formulating a response to the congressional directive. To specifically answer Congress, the methodology must be applied on a billet-by-billet basis to all positions identified as potential Joint Duty Assignments. This section presents the results of applying the methodology to the census data.[1]

We first discuss the implications of applying the Joint Time/Joint Function algorithm under the restrictions imposed by law and by DoD policy. We then examine the impact of relaxing the DoD policy of restricting O-3 positions from the JDAL and of changing the law to allow selected in-service positions to receive joint duty credit. Finally, we describe an analytical approach for identifying critical billets and present the results of applying the approach to the census data.

Implications Under Current Law and DoD Policy

We first consider the implications of the two potential new JDALs (4900 and 7200 based on the 12,000 processed surveys in Table 2.4) under the current law and DoD policy. Figure 3.1 shows for each organizational grouping the percentage of billets we processed (excluding all O-3 billets) that would be on a new JDAL using algorithm 2. The leftmost bar in each group shows the percentage of the processed billets (above the grade of O-3) that are currently on the JDAL. These percentages closely match the current 100 percent/50 percent rule. The middle bar in each group is based on the breakpoint containing the first three groups (scores of 4.0 or higher). The rightmost bar in each group is based on a JDAL composed from the first two groups (scores of 5.8 or higher).

For the new list that is approximately the same size as the current list (i.e., the list based on the first three groups), the 100 percent organizations such as the Joint Staff and the Unified Commands all lose positions on the JDAL. The defense agencies and some other 50 percent organizations gain positions. For the smaller

---

[1]Results are presented for the 12,000 billets we processed. There are approximately 3000 billets whose responses have not been either received or processed. These additional 3000 billets must be considered in the ultimate size and composition of a new JDAL.

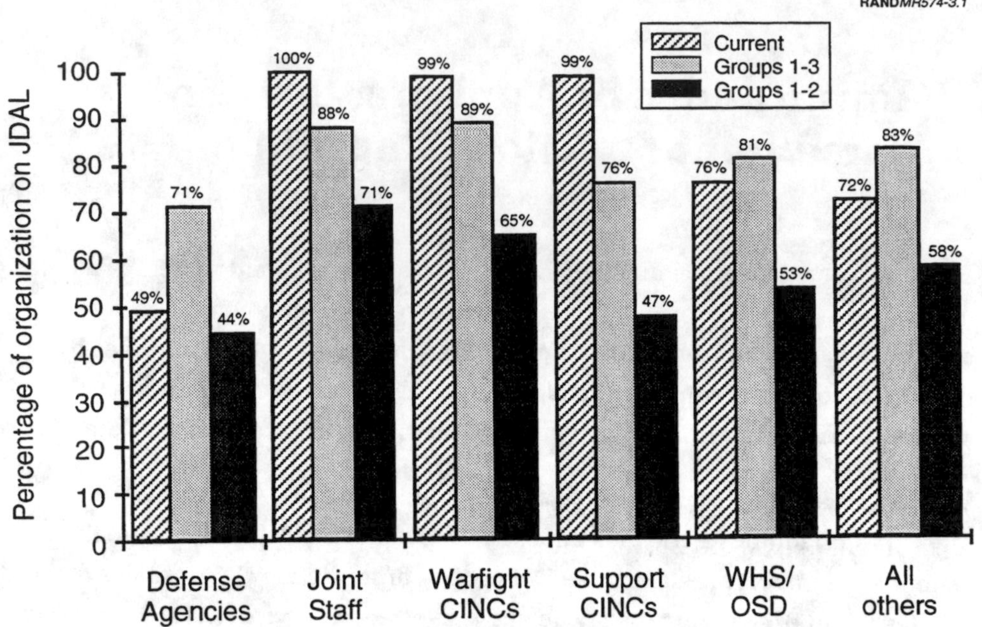

Figure 3.1—Percentage of Processed Billets on a JDAL Using Algorithm 2

list, all organizations lose positions on the JDAL, with the current 100 percent organizations feeling the largest impact.

Although the percentage of billets on the JDAL for defense agencies is shown as a single value, the percentages for different defense agencies vary widely, as shown in Figure 3.2. At the low end, approximately 25 percent of the billets at the Defense Finance and Accounting Service (DFAS) would be on the JDAL based on the first three groups, while over 80 percent of the billets at the Defense Intelligence Agency (DIA) would be on the same list.

Figure 3.3 shows the number of positions by military service[2] on the current JDAL and on each of the new lists. The distribution of joint billets by service for the larger of the two new lists (the middle bar) is very similar to the distribution of the current JDAL.

Figure 3.4 shows similar results by the grade required for the position. The new list that is approximately the same size as the current list shows a slight increase in the grade of O-4, with decreases in the higher grades.

[2]The distinctions by service, grade, and skill are all based on the stated *requirements* for the position and not on the attributes of the individual filling the position.

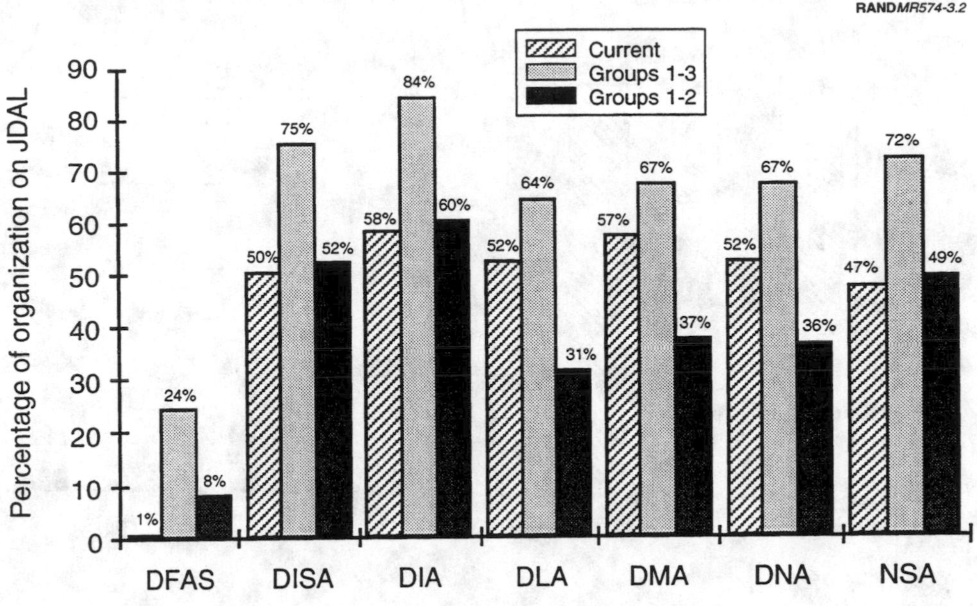

Figure 3.2—Percentage of Defense Agency Positions

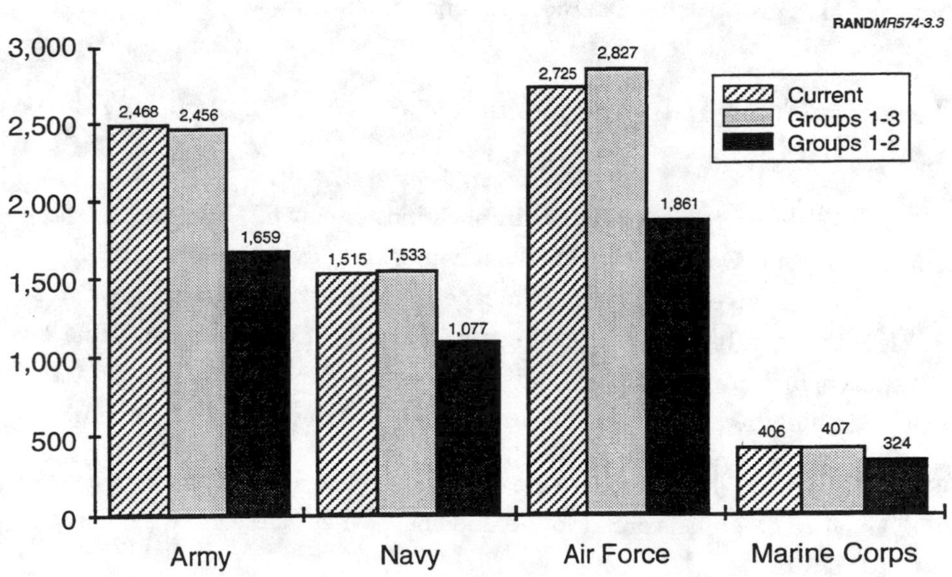

Figure 3.3—Number of Positions by Military Service

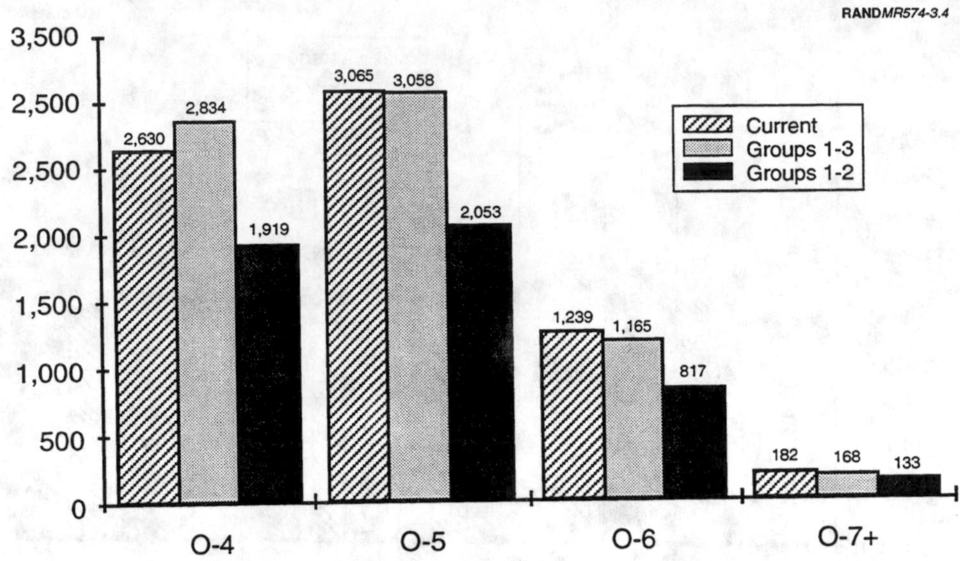

Figure 3.4—Number of Positions by Grade

Finally, Figure 3.5 portrays the distribution of the current and two new JDALs by selected skill group using DoD occupational codes.[3]

Implications If Current Policy Were Changed to Allow O-3 Billets

Figures 3.1 through 3.5 portray the implications of new JDALs based on the current law and DoD policy. What is the impact on these new JDALs if DoD policy were changed to allow O-3s to receive joint credit where appropriate? Table 3.1 shows the results of adding the O-3s to the total we saw in Table 2.4. As shown, including O-3 billets increases the size of the smaller new JDAL by approximately 17 percent and the larger new JDAL by around 18 percent.

Figures 3.6 through 3.8 compare the current JDAL to the two potential new JDALs when O-3 billets are included and show where these increases come from.

---

[3]These codes, maintained by the Defense Manpower Data Center, map service skills to DoD occupations. Most are self-explanatory. Engineering and Maintenance includes communications and some data processing (generally hardware-related). Scientists and Professionals includes educators and instructors. Supply, Procurement, and Allied includes officers in transportation, services, and related logistics activities who are not classified elsewhere. Administrators include data processing (generally software and information-related). We have not included three skill groups: Health Care and Non-Occupational (because of small numbers), and General Officers (because their numbers were shown in Figure 3.4).

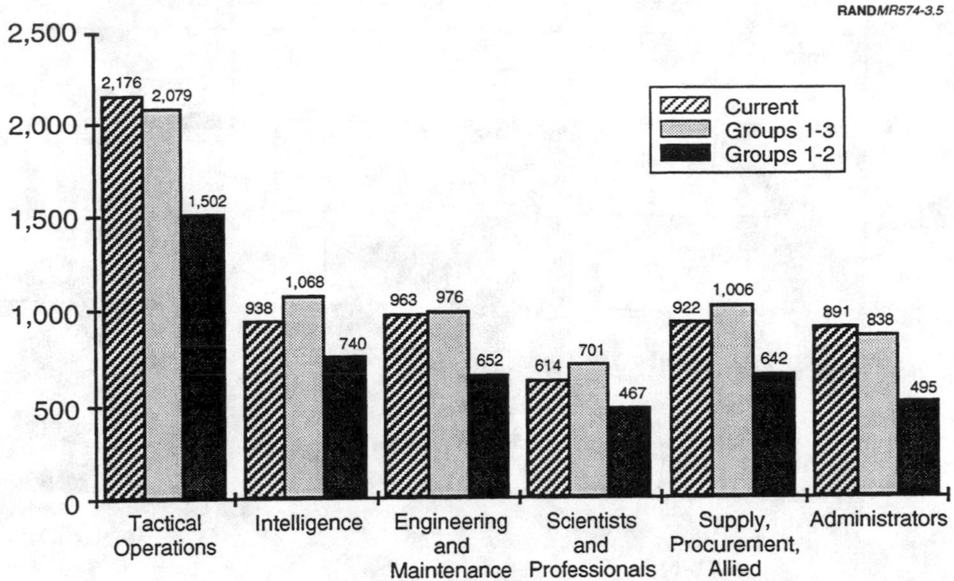

Figure 3.5—Number of Positions by Selected Skill Group

Table 3.1

Size of New JDALs Based on Scoring Algorithm, Including O-3 Billets (Based on 12,000 Surveys Processed)

Restriction	Current JDAL	New JDAL Based on Groups 1–2	New JDAL Based on Groups 1–3
Current law and policy	7200	4900	7200
Including O-3 billets	—	850	1300
Total JDAL	7200	5750	8500

Figure 3.6 shows the number of billets on the current and two new JDALs for each organizational grouping. The organization of the bars is the same as before, with the current JDAL on the left, the larger of the two new JDALs in the middle, and the JDAL based on the first two groups on the right. The shaded portions of the center and right bars correspond to the O-3 billets in each group.

Allowing O-3s to receive joint credit has the biggest impact on the defense agencies, the Unified Commands, and several of the "other" organizations, with little or no effect on the Joint Staff or the Office of the Secretary of Defense (because the latter two organizations have no or few O-3 positions).

Figure 3.7 shows the number of billets on the current and each of the new JDALs by military service when O-3 billets are allowed to receive joint credit. The biggest percentage impact is for the Air Force and the Navy.

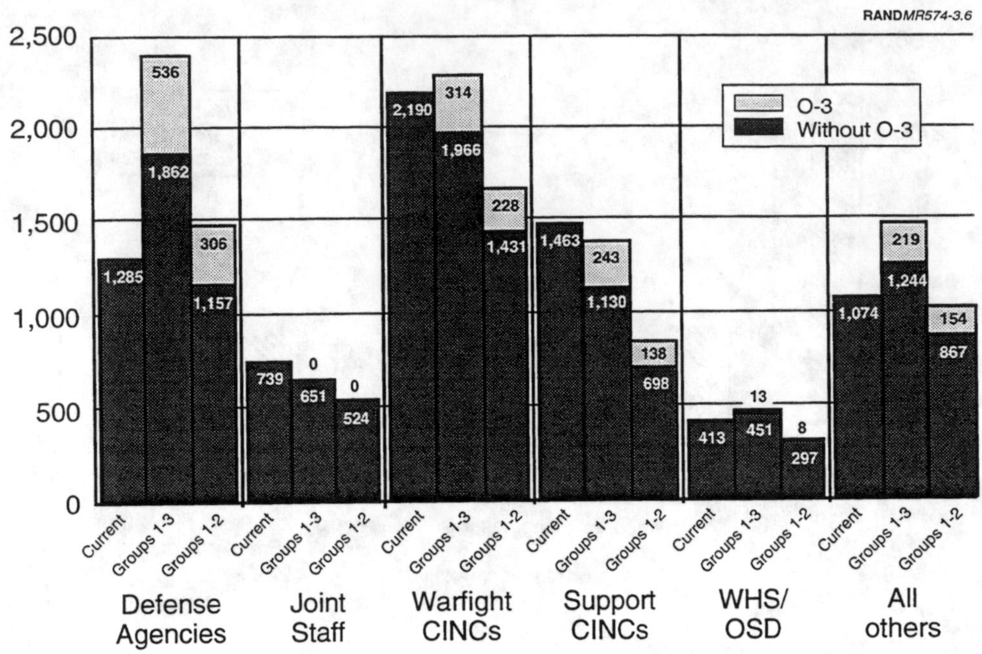

Figure 3.6—Number of Positions by Organization Including Grade O-3

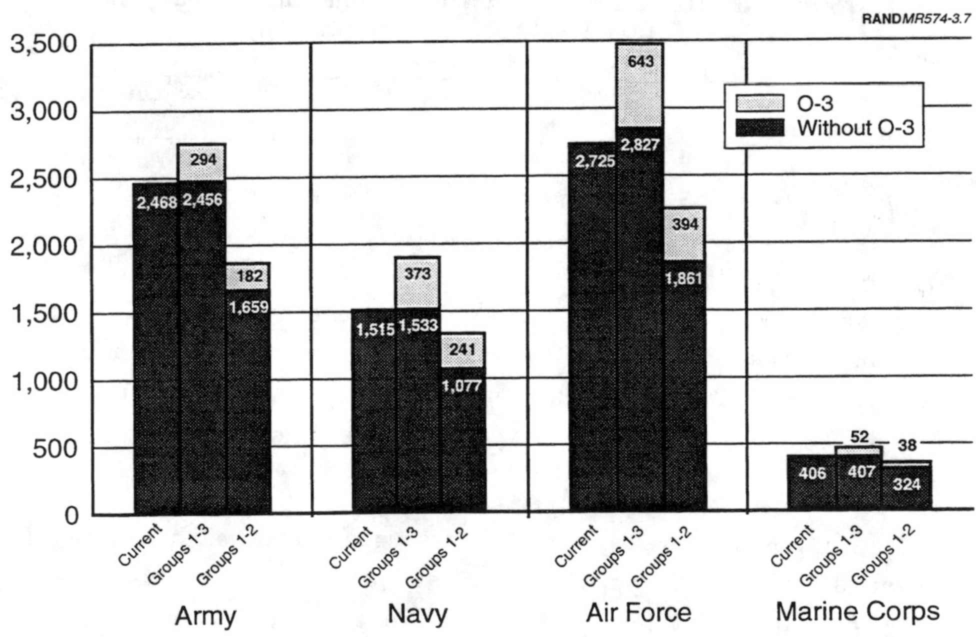

Figure 3.7—Number of Positions on JDAL by Service Including Grade O-3

Finally, Figure 3.8 shows the impact of allowing O-3s to receive joint credit by skill classification. The biggest impact by far is in the Intelligence functional area.

From the services's perspective, there are several advantages to allowing O-3 positions to receive joint credit. The law states that approximately 50 percent of the positions *for grades above O-3* must be filled by Joint Specialty Officers (JSOs) or JSO nominees (JSO noms). Adding O-3 positions to the JDAL does not increase the number of officers that must complete Joint Professional Military Education (JPME) Phase II or the number of JSOs needed by the services. Also, the opportunity to receive joint credit when serving in a position as an O-3 increases the number of officers who have the joint duty requirement for promotion to general or flag officer. Unfortunately, there would be a lengthy period between serving a joint tour as an O-3 and being promoted to the general/flag rank.

There may also be disadvantages to allowing O-3s to receive joint credit. Under current promotion objectives, the services would have to carefully manage the O-3 officers sent to joint positions. However, the promotion rate from O-3 to O-4 is approximately 80 percent, so the management burden may not be substantial. In MR-593-JS, we discuss the possibility of excluding O-3s from the Goldwater-Nichols promotion comparisons.

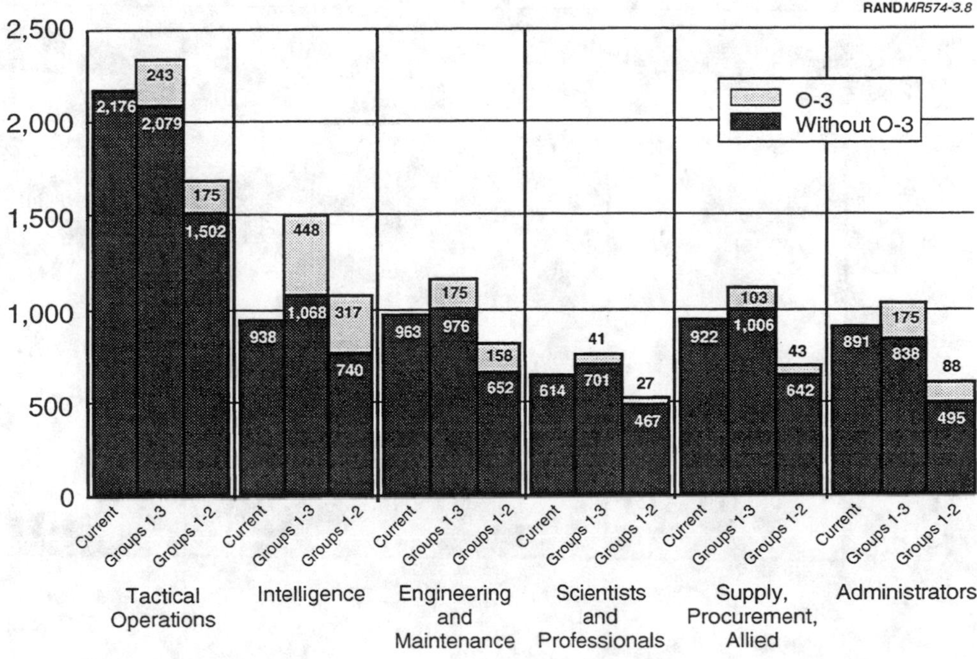

Figure 3.8—Number of Positions on JDAL by Skill Group Including Grade O-3

Implications If Current Law Were Changed to Allow In-Service Positions

What if the law were modified to allow certain in-service billets to receive joint credit? Table 3.2, which builds off of Table 3.1, shows the impact of allowing the in-service billets. Adding in in-service billets increases the smaller new JDAL by around 24 percent and the larger new JDAL by approximately 29 percent.

Figures 3.9, 3.10, and 3.11 show these results by service, grade, and skill group, respectively. Most of the in-service billets with high joint scores are in the O-4 to O-6 grades and are primarily in the Tactical Operations and the Supply, Procurement, and Allied skill areas.

Table 3.2

Size of New JDALs Based on Scoring Algorithm, Including O-3s and In-Service Billets (Based on 12,000 Surveys Processed)

Restriction	Current JDAL	New JDAL Based on Groups 1–2	New JDAL Based on Groups 1–3
Current law and policy	7200	4900	7200
Including O-3 billets	—	850	1300
Including in-service billets	—	350	800
Total JDAL	7200	6100	9300

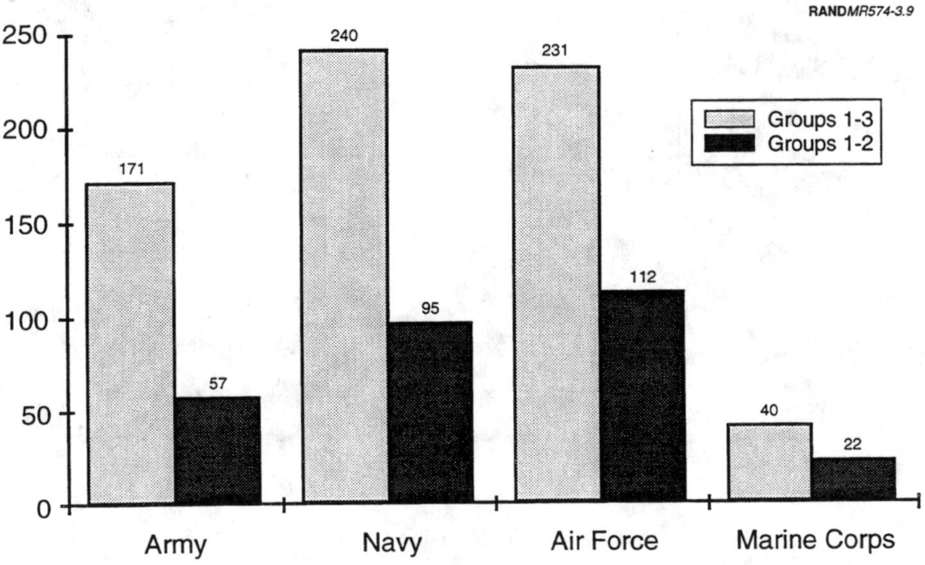

Figure 3.9—In-Service Positions Added to JDAL by Service

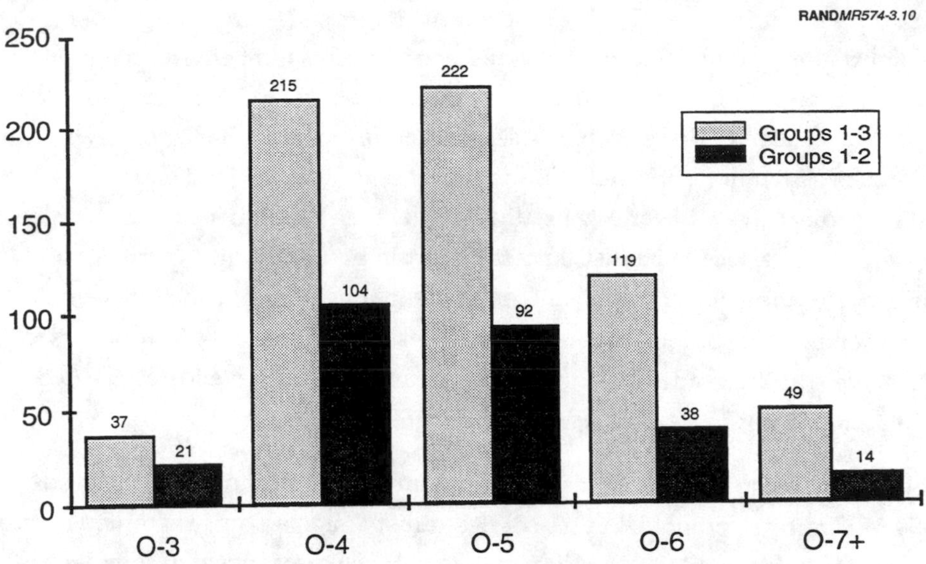

Figure 3.10—In-Service Positions Added to JDAL by Grade

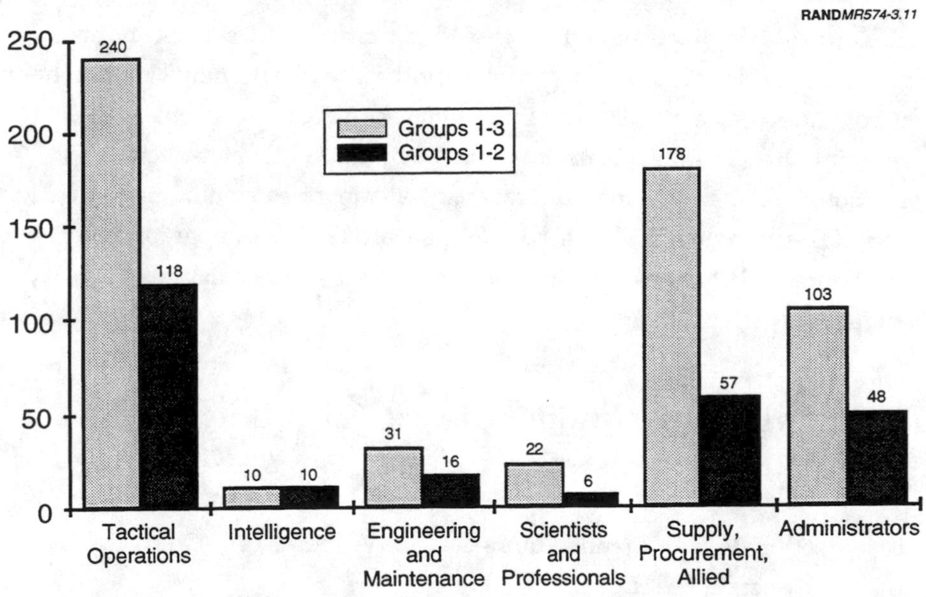

Figure 3.11—In-Service Positions Added to JDAL by Skill Group

Changing the law to permit selected in-service positions to qualify for joint credit would benefit the services by allowing officers to acquire their joint duty requirement for promotion to general/flag officer without serving a tour outside of their service organizations. However, the in-service billets that might qualify for joint credit should possibly be limited to the grades of O-4 to O-6.

Joint duty billets have at least two aspects of "jointness"—providing experience in joint matters and providing that experience within a joint environment or culture. From our analysis of the survey data, some in-service billets provide joint experience but do so within a "service" environment. Our interviews with various organizations and senior leaders suggested that the joint experience for O-3s is typically at a lower organizational level than for higher grades. Therefore, in-service O-3 billets may fall short in both the joint experience and the joint environment aspects of a joint assignment. Furthermore, the services identified few O-3 billets for consideration (less than 5 percent of the in-service billets were at the grade of O-3). For these reasons, we believe in-service O-3 billets should not be designated as Joint Duty Assignments.

Goldwater-Nichols mandates a prior joint tour before promotion to the grade of O-7. Waivers are granted, but the services must assign an officer granted such a waiver almost immediately to a joint tour. In those cases, the joint tour for a general/flag officer without prior joint experience should be outside of his or her own service. Therefore, we believe in-service billets that qualify for joint credit should be for grades below O-7.

Adding in-service billets would increase the number of JSOs or JSO noms required by the services and, therefore, would place an additional burden on the joint education system. Also, in-service billets could cause a problem in developing the promotion statistics required by the Goldwater-Nichols legislation. For example, in which category or categories would one place a joint qualified position on a service headquarters staff? In the companion report, we discuss potential changes to the promotion comparison calculations that may alleviate any such problem.

Determining the Number of Critical Billets

Background

As discussed in Section 1 (and in more detail in Appendix A), Goldwater-Nichols requires the Secretary of Defense to

> designate not fewer than 1,000 joint duty assignment positions as critical joint duty assignment positions. Such designation shall be made by examining each joint duty assignment position and designating under the preceding sentence those positions for which, considering the duties and

> responsibilities of the position, it is highly important that the occupant be particularly trained in, and oriented towards, joint matters.[4]

Currently, all critical positions must be filled by JSOs, unless the Secretary of Defense or the Chairman of the Joint Chiefs of Staff grants a waiver on a case-by-case basis.

The basis for the requirement of at least 1000 critical positions is unclear. One objective of the Goldwater-Nichols legislation may have been to ensure that an adequate precentage of the officers assigned to joint duty positions had joint experience. Since critical billets must be filled with officers who have had joint experience, the number of critical billets dictates the minimum number of joint experienced officers serving in joint organizations. Currently, services tend to use JSOs almost exclusively in critical billets. Therefore, reducing the number of critical billets is likely to reduce the average experience level of officers serving in joint organizations and the number of JSOs in the services.

Other than the statement that "the occupant be trained in and oriented towards joint matters," the law provides no guidelines on how to identify critical positions. Currently, each organization is allocated a number of critical positions on a fair-share basis. The individual organizations then determine which of their joint duty positions should be designated as critical.

A Methodology for Determining the Number of Critical Billets

One of the goals of our research was to develop an objective approach for identifying joint critical positions and to apply the approach to the survey data.

Determining Filters. The first step was to define what constitutes a critical position. Although the law is not definitive in this regard, the requirement that JSOs fill all critical positions provides a starting point.

To become a JSO candidate, an officer must as a general rule complete JPME Phase II and then serve a joint duty tour. With the completion of these two prerequisites, an officer can be nominated by his or her service for selection by the Secretary of Defense to be designated a JSO. Therefore, two attributes of critical positions are that the officer assigned to the position must have completed JPME Phase II and must have previously served in a joint duty position.

---

[4]Section 661(d)(2)(A), Chapter 38, Title 10, United States Code (as amended through December 31, 1992), April 1993, U.S. Government Printing Office, Washington, DC.

Another constraint on critical positions is the required grade of the officer assigned to the position. Because of the education and previous joint experience requirements for a JSO, it is unlikely that an officer will become a JSO before he or she attains the grade of O-5. Therefore, critical positions should be limited to those that require an officer at the O-5 level or higher.

Finally, the law suggests that a position's duties and responsibilities are important when determining critical positions. One interpretation of this distinction is that certain types of functional duties (e.g., positions providing administrative support) should be excluded from consideration as a designated critical position.[5]

In summary, then, the four conditions listed above—completion of JPME, completion of previous tour of duty, a grade of O-5 or higher, and the elimination of certain positions—serve as "filters" or attributes a position must possess before it can be further considered as a critical position candidate. Therefore, these filters serve to narrow our list to those that may qualify as critical positions.

We are not suggesting that these are the only filters that could be used to determine candidates for critical billets. However, we believe they represent a reasonable method for eliminating a subset of all billets from contention. More important, we believe an objective method for identifying critical billets must begin with rules that define a set of attributes for critical positions. The rules do not necessarily identify those billets that should be designated as critical as much as they eliminate some billets from consideration.

Scoring the Filtered Billets. After applying the filters to the survey data, a set of positions remains for further evaluation. We judge these remaining positions based on their joint content. Our methodology for measuring the joint content of a position leads us to believe that two important attributes of critical positions are the amount of time spent on matters involving multiple services or other nations (Joint Time) and the nature of the duties and responsibilities of the position when working on matters of a joint nature (Joint Function).

We include a third measure of joint content in our methodology for determining critical billets. Because JSOs must fill critical billets, and because JSOs have a broad perspective and a degree of continuity in the joint arena from their joint training and prior experience, we believe critical billets should involve some degree of data synthesis and decisionmaking. That is, a critical billet should not

[5]This filter was based on the response to the survey's question 10, which asked respondents to characterize the nature of their billet based on a list of several generic characterizations.

just supply information to others but should also receive information and have responsibility for reviewing that information and making appropriate decisions. We call this criterion "Joint Decisionmaking."[6]

The filters identified previously were of an "either-or" nature. That is, the attributes of a position had to satisfy the stated conditions to pass through and become a candidate for a critical billet. The three measures of joint content—Joint Time, Joint Function, and Joint Decisionmaking—are different. They are more like "dials" than "filters."

Demonstrating the Critical Billet Methodology. By setting the joint content "dials" at different values, fewer or more billets will be identified as critical. As an example, Table 3.3 shows the resulting number of critical billets after the various filters and specific settings for the joint content "dials" are applied. Table 3.4 shows the impact of setting the joint content "dials" at different values.

Figures 3.12 and 3.13 show the distribution of critical billets for the example shown in Table 3.3. Figure 3.12 shows the percentage (and number) of critical billets for each organizational grouping. Each bar represents the percentage of the billets processed that would be critical using the values specified in Table 3.3. The numbers of critical billets are shown in the inset.

Table 3.3

Example of Critical Billet Methodology (Based on 12,000 Billets Processed)

Rules	Number of Positions
Filters:	
Number of billets processed	12,026
Require JPME II	5,246[a]
Require previous joint tour	3,011
Grade O-5 or higher	1,892
Eliminate certain types of positions	1,735
SCORES:	
Joint Time ≥ 50%	1,184
Joint Function ≥ 5	892
Joint Decisionmaking ≥ 25%	502

[a]The values for number of positions are the billets remaining after each filter is applied successively. That is, of the 12,026 surveys processed, 5,246 passed through the first filter.Of those 5,246, 3,011 passed through the second filter, and so forth.

[6]We based the score for this measure on responses to question 15.

Table 3.4

Effect on Number of Critical Billets of Adjusting Values for Joint Content Variables (Based on 12,000 Billets Processed)

Joint Time Score	Joint Function Score	Joint Decisionmaking Score	Number of Positions
50%	5.0	25%	502
50%	5.0	33%	341
50%	5.0	50%	227
58%	5.8	25%	346
58%	5.8	33%	233
58%	5.8	50%	164

NOTE: Scores are all greater than or equal to the value shown.

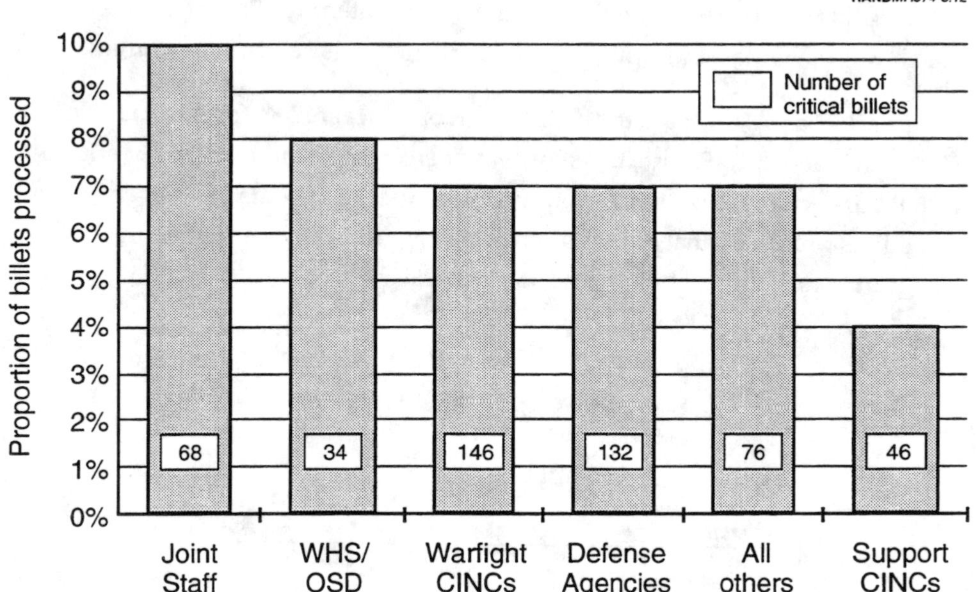

Figure 3.12—Critical Billets By Organization

Figure 3.13 shows the distribution of critical billets for this example by service and by grade. Although some services have greater numbers of critical billets, the critical billets are relatively evenly distributed by service on a percentage basis. Higher grades have greater proportions of critical billets even though the numbers of them are fewer.

Analysis Results. Our analysis of critical billets suggests that a systematic approach for determining which joint billets are designated as critical is preferred

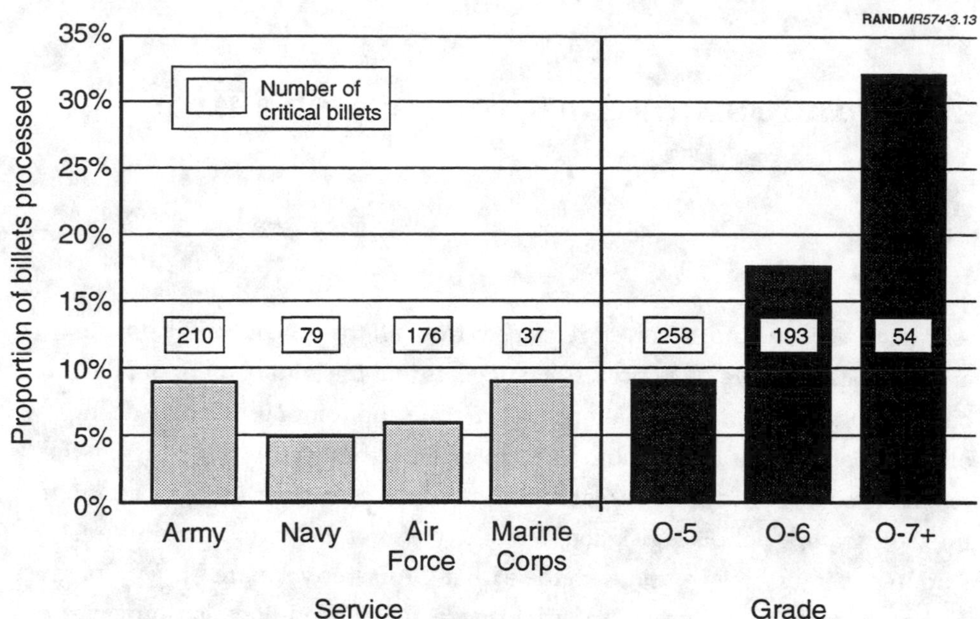

Figure 3.13—Critical Billets by Service and Grade

to the subjective methods currently used. Using reasonable filters and values for appropriate criteria results in fewer—potentially many fewer—critical billets than the 1000 figure stated in Goldwater-Nichols.

4. Conclusions and Recommendations

Conclusions

Although we have not received responses from all the candidate billets, the analysis of billets we have processed suggests that the joint content of billets can be measured using a combination of Joint Time and Joint Function. Adding other variables results in a more complex relationship with little change in the resulting scores or rankings. Our methodology is consistent with the intent of the Goldwater-Nichols legislation, with the views of the various senior-level leaders we interviewed, and with the earlier GAO study referred to by Congress in their tasking of the research. Furthermore, the methodology is simple yet logical and based solely on the joint content of a position.

Applying the methodology enabled us to rank-order the positions based on the resulting scores. Several breakpoints in the ordered list are possible, although a degree of subjectivity is associated with any of them. Because of this subjectivity, the size of the new JDAL should be determined in conjunction with the number of joint positions that can be supported by the military services. (The results of that analysis are presented in MR-593-JS, *How Many Can Be Joint? Supporting Joint Duty Assignments.*)

Regardless of where the ordered list is "cut" to form a new JDAL, the following statements can be made:

- Virtually all of the candidate billets have some joint content associated with them.
- Based purely on the joint content algorithm, no organization will have all its positions on a new JDAL[1] (i.e., there will be no 100 percent organizations unless a policy decision dictates that all the applicable billets in specific organizations be granted joint duty credit).
- Defense agencies will not uniformly have 50 percent of their positions on a new JDAL, as is the case with the current implementation of Goldwater-Nichols. Some defense agencies will have a far lower percentage, while

[1]Organizations with only certain positions receiving joint credit may experience morale problems among the officers assigned to those organizations. Responses to question 27 on the survey indicates such morale problems would exist (see Appendix D).

others will have a much higher percentage of their positions indicated as JDAs.

- Some O-3 and in-service positions have significant joint content. Including these positions on a new JDAL would require changing the law and current DoD policy.
- Using a systematic approach to determining which positions are "critical joint billets" is preferred to the subjective approach currently used by organizations. Based on reasonable criteria values, there are likely to be fewer, potentially many fewer, critical billets than the 1000 figure stated in the Goldwater-Nichols legislation.

Recommendations

Based on these findings, we make the following recommendations:

- **Use the Joint Time/Joint Function algorithm to produce a joint content score for each billet.** Use the resulting scores to produce an ordered list from most joint content to least joint content. Determine the size of a new JDAL (i.e., where to "cut" the ordered list) based on the number of joint positions the services can support (see MR-593-JS). This will produce an initial minimum score for a billet to qualify for joint credit. For example, if the new JDAL has approximately the same number of positions as the current JDAL, joint scores of 4.0 or higher would be considered for joint credit (assuming the current law and policy of excluding in-service and O-3 billets). Closely examine, using comparisons with similar billets and inputs from organizational commanders, the ten percent of the billets that lie above and below the minimum score to make final determinations on which positions are placed on a new JDAL.
- **Consider changing the DoD policy to allow O-3s to receive joint credit.** There are advantages and disadvantages associated with allowing O-3 positions on the JDAL. Further examine these advantages and disadvantages, especially in light of any proposed changes to the Goldwater-Nichols promotion comparisons.
- **Request changes to Goldwater-Nichols to:**
  - — Allow in-service billets for grades of O-4 to O-6;
  - — Employ a specific methodology for identifying critical billets.

Appendix

A. Overview of Goldwater-Nichols

This appendix provides an overview of the personnel provisions of the Goldwater-Nichols legislation. It describes the concerns that led to Title IV, highlights the general features of the personnel portion of the law, and defines some of the terms used throughout the report. The section also describes the DoD implementation of Goldwater-Nichols and shows the size and distribution of the current Joint Duty Assignment List (JDAL).

Background to Goldwater-Nichols: Concerns About Officers

Barry Goldwater states in his autobiography[1] that military experiences in World War II showed him that the military services did not work well together. More recent problems with joint operations, such as the failed hostage rescue mission in Iran and the invasion of Grenada, led him to seriously examine joint service capabilities. The common perception of the time, supported by the testimony of numerous witnesses in the hearings that led to the passage of Goldwater-Nichols,[2] was that the military services had little respect for joint service or for assignments outside their individual service organizations. The services typically sent second-rate officers to such assignments and removed them as quickly as possible. Joint assignments were not desired by military officers, who viewed them as a hindrance in their career progression.

The authors of Goldwater-Nichols felt that military officers, especially the general and flag officers,[3] had little understanding or appreciation of the policies, procedures, operations, or capabilities of the other services. As a result, they had little experience in or knowledge of the conduct of joint operations. Realizing that future contingencies would almost always involve two or more military services acting together, the authors of Goldwater-Nichols felt strongly that

---

[1]Barry M. Goldwater and Jack Casserly, *Goldwater*, Doubleday, New York, 1988 (especially Chapter 11, Duty-Honor-Country, pp. 334–361).

[2]99th Congress—1st Session, *Defense Organization: The Need for Change*, Senate Print 99-86, Committee on Armed Services, United States Senate, October 16, 1985 and 99th Congress, 2nd Session, *Reorganization of the Department of Defense, Hearings Before the Investigations Subcommittee on Armed Services*, HASC No. 99-53, House of Representatives, 1987.

[3]The officer corps is typically divided into three groups by pay grade: company grade (O-1 [lieutenants and ensigns] to O-3 [captains and Navy lieutenants]), field grade (O-4 [majors and lieutenant commanders] to O-6 [colonels and Navy captains]), and general/flag (O-7 to O-10).

something had to be done to instill a joint culture (i.e., attitudes, values, and beliefs about joint service) among the officer corps, a culture that would lead to an appreciation and understanding of how the services could and should operate together in future conflicts. To us, this is the main intent of Goldwater-Nichols and guides much of our analysis on determining which positions should be designated as Joint Duty Assignments. It is significant that, eight years after the passage of Goldwater-Nichols, individual officers have accepted the reality of a joint culture and the need for certain joint assignments as a necessity for the most successful careers.[4]

Personnel Provisions of Goldwater-Nichols

The personnel provisions of the DoD Reorganization Act of 1986[5] can be described as a reaction to existing concerns, and an effort to

- Increase the quality of officers in joint assignments;
- Enhance the stability and increase the joint experience of officers in joint assignments;
- Enhance the education and training of officers in joint matters and strengthen the focus of professional military education in preparing officers for Joint Duty Assignment positions;
- Ensure that general/flag officers are well-rounded in joint matters;
- Ensure that officers are not disadvantaged by joint service.

Title 10 defined *joint matters* as "matters relating to the integrated employment of land, sea, and air forces, including matters relating to national military strategy; strategic planning and contingency planning; and command and control of combat operations under unified command."[6] The law required that the Secretary of Defense define the term "joint duty assignment" and limit the definition to assignments in which an officer "gains a significant experience in joint matters." It specifically excluded assignments for joint training or joint education and assignments within an officer's own military department. Finally,

---

[4]This observation is based on interviews conducted during the study and on responses to opinion questions in the survey (Appendix D). In particular, only 18 percent of officer respondents and 7 percent of general/flag officer respondents did not believe their present joint assignment would contribute significantly to their performance in future service assignments.

[5]99th Congress, Second Session, *Department of Defense Reorganization Act of 1986*, P.L. 99-433, in United States Code Congressional and Administrative News, Volume 1, West Publishing Co., St. Paul, Minn., 1986, Title IV—Joint Officer Personnel Policy.

[6]Section 668(a), Chapter 38, Title 10, United States Code (as amended through December 31, 1992), April 1993, U.S. Government Printing Office, Washington, DC.

the law required the Secretary of Defense to publish a list, termed the Joint Duty Assignment List, showing the positions that qualify as Joint Duty Assignments (JDAs).

Goldwater-Nichols created a new category of officers termed Joint Specialty Officers (JSOs). These officers were to be "particularly trained in, and oriented towards, joint matters." Prerequisites to becoming a JSO included successfully completing a program at a Joint Professional Military Education (JPME)[7] school and then serving a full tour in a Joint Duty Assignment. Once these two prerequisites were met, the officer's military service could "nominate" them for "selection" as a JSO. Final selection rested with the Secretary of Defense with the advice of the Chairman of the Joint Chiefs of Staff. The law stipulated that at least half of the positions on the JDAL *above the grade of O-3* be filled by JSOs or officers nominated as JSOs (termed JSO noms).[8]

Title IV specified that the Secretary designate at least 1000 of the positions on the JDAL as Critical Joint Duty Assignments (CJDAs). These positions were to be identified by examining each joint duty position and designating those for which, considering the duties and responsibilities of the position, it was "highly important that the occupant be particularly trained in, and oriented toward, joint matters." Initially, 80 percent of the positions were to be filled by JSOs, but by January 1, 1994, JSOs were to be assigned to all critical positions.

Title IV specified that the duration of JDA tours average at least three and one-half years for field grade officers and at least three years for general and flag officers. These tour lengths were later amended to three years for field grade officers and two years for general and flag officers.

Title IV provided special considerations for "warfighters." It specified that the Secretary of Defense identify "critical occupational specialties" (COSs) whose officers were directly connected with combat arms (or analogous operations), and who needed to concentrate on developing, maintaining, and then passing on to others specific warfighting skills. The services had argued strongly that these skills were critical and complex, and that time away from such operational (i.e., service) billets would quickly cause those skills to deteriorate.

---

[7]JPME Phase I is part of intermediate- or senior-level courses at the service colleges. JPME Phase II is provided by the Armed Forces Staff College in a three-month, resident-only course. The National War College and the Industrial College of the Armed Forces provide both JPME Phase I and Phase II in their ten-month resident courses.

[8]JSO nominees have either (1) successfully completed JPME but not yet served a full JDA tour or (2) a military occupational specialty that has been designated as a critical occupational specialty involving combat operations.

Officers with a COS were allowed to leave their initial joint assignment after 24 months. That two-year assignment would fulfill the tour requirement for JSO and, as will be discussed shortly, it would fulfill the JDA tour requirement for appointment to general or flag officer. COS officers were also permitted to reverse the order of the prerequisites needed to become a JSO. That is, COS officers could first serve in a JDA and then attend a JPME school.[9]

Finally, the law specified that a prior JDA was a prerequisite for promotion to general or flag officer. It did allow, for a period of time, selected waivers to this requirement.

The law did include provisions for a phase-in period. If JDAs were just being specified, it was not reasonable to expect that 50 percent of the officers filling them could have already completed a prior tour. The transition provisions stated that the JDAL should be published within six months, and that filling half of all the critical billets by JSOs should be implemented "as rapidly as possible, and not later than two years after the date of the enactment of the act." Congress did allow the services to select a number of "transition" JSOs based on their prior duties and experience. These transition JSOs initially filled the critical billets and still remain a large segment of all the JSOs within the individual services.

Promotion Policy Objectives of Goldwater-Nichols

Title IV contained "protections" written into the law that officers sent to joint duty would in fact be "quality" officers and that after they completed their joint duty assignments they would not be penalized in any way by their services. These protections took the form of promotion rate comparisons. The law specified that the promotion rate be as follows:

- Officers holding the designation of JSO should average at least as high as the average of officers in the same service and competitive group who were serving or had served on the service headquarters staff.
- Officers who were serving on, or had served on, the Joint Staff should meet the same standard.[10]

---

[9]Non-COS officers could also attain JSO status by first completing a joint tour and then attending JPME. Any officer could also qualify by serving two complete JDA tours. Both of these paths to becoming a JSO require a waiver by the Secretary of Defense. The educational requirement could be waived if the Secretary of Defense determined that it was impractical for the officer to complete JPME at the current stage of his or her career and that the types of JDAs completed by the officer were "of sufficient breadth to prepare the officer adequately for the joint specialty."

[10]By policy, officers who were serving in or had served in the Office of the Secretary of Defense should also meet this standard.

- Officers who were serving in, or had served in, other JDAs should average at least as high as the service-wide average for officers in the same service and competitive group.

The law requires that the Secretary of Defense provide a report to Congress, on at least a semi-annual basis, on the promotion rates of officers in the various categories outlined above. If the promotion rates fail to meet the legal objectives, the Secretary must provide information on specific failures and describe actions or plans to prevent future failures.

These promotion objectives are most often mentioned by the services as the main problem they face in meeting the stipulations of Goldwater-Nichols. Furthermore, the "rules" for the promotion comparisons are complex and not well understood by the various services. The basis for comparison is not consistently applied across the services or over time in a specific service. This "supportability" issue is discussed in MR-593-JS, *How Many Can Be Joint? Supporting Joint Duty Assignments.*

DoD Implementation of Goldwater-Nichols

Most of the provisions written into Title IV were not really new. As a 1990 DoD study of its provisions stated: "Almost every provision can be traced back to specific problems, both real and perceived, noted by the Congress over the past forty years. Many provisions that became law existed in DoD policy directives prior to 1986; however, Congress was convinced that these directives were not rigorously followed . . . ."[11]

The law required the Secretary of Defense to define the term Joint Duty Assignment and to publish a Joint Duty Assignment List of positions that qualify as JDAs. The Secretary of Defense defined a *joint duty assignment* as

> an assignment to a designated position in a multi-Service or multinational command or activity that is involved in the integrated employment or support of the land, sea, and air forces of at least two of the three Military Departments. Such involvement includes, but is not limited to, matters relating to national military strategy, joint doctrine and policy, strategic planning, contingency planning, and command and control of combat operations under a unified command.[12]

---

[11]Office of the Secretary of Defense (Force Management and Personnel), *Report on the Study of Joint Officer Management Initiatives*, draft, April 1990, p. 28.

[12]Joint Chiefs of Staff, *Joint Officer Management*, JCS Administrative Publication 1.2, Washington, DC, June 1989.

The original implementation of the law, and the one that is still being used today, reflects somewhat of a compromise aimed at producing a JDAL of approximately 8000 positions. Part of the problem was the degree of uncertainty and subjectivity surrounding the definitions of joint matters and JDAs. A rather broad-brush approach was taken. Joint assignments were limited to grades of O-4 (major or lieutenant commander) and higher. This limitation was a DoD policy, since the law specifically allowed O-3s (captains and Navy lieutenants) to be considered for joint duty credit.

All of the positions at the grades of O-4 and above at the Joint Staff, the Office of the Secretary of Defense, and the unified commands were placed on the JDAL. Half of the positions at each defense agency were permitted joint credit. The specific defense agency positions on the JDAL were identified by each agency. Finally, the 1000 critical billets were allocated on more or less a fair share basis to the above organizations. Each organization identified the specific billets to be considered critical.

The current JDAL has grown to more than 9000 positions. The specific billets on the list change constantly as organizations add or delete positions. Table A.1 shows the composition of the JDAL by service and grade as of November 1994. The distribution by different type activities for the same time period is shown in Table A.2.

Table A.1

Composition of the JDAL by Service and Pay Grade

Grade	USA	USN	USAF	USMC	Total
O–4	1103	679	1330	197	3309
O–5	1390	792	1416	246	3844
O–6	602	397	743	74	1716
O–7+	75	61	78	12	234
Total	3170	1929	3467	529	9103

SOURCE: JDAL 94-1, as of November 1994.

Table A.2

Critical Joint Positions by Activity

Activity	Joint Positions	Critical Joint Positions	Percent of Present Joint Positions that Are Critical
Combatant commands	4950	513	10.3
Joint staff	766	90	11.7
OSD	406	25	6.1
Defense agencies	1925	234	12.1
Other joint activities	822	50	6.1
Generals/admirals	234	97	41.4
Total	9103	1009	11.1

SOURCE: JDAL 94-1, as of November 1994.

B. Survey Questionnaire

RCS JCS (OT) 1933 February 22, 1994

1994 JOINT DUTY ASSIGNMENT SURVEY

PURPOSE:

- The Congress, in the 1993 National Defense Authorization Act, directed the Secretary of Defense to review the appropriateness of positions included on the Joint Duty Assignment List (JDAL).
- The Director for Manpower and Personnel (J1), the Joint Staff, has asked RAND and the Logistics Management Institute (two not-for-profit, federally funded research and development centers) to conduct an independent study regarding the nature and content of the Joint Duty Assignment List.
- As part of this study, we are conducting a survey of all officers in pay grades O3 and higher who are assigned to positions in the Joint Staff, OSD, Unified Commands, Defense Agencies and activities and selected positions within each Service.
- The survey is designed to collect information about your current organization; your military background, training, and experience; your current position and the work you perform; and your opinions on selected topics.
- The information you provide in this survey will be used to develop alternative future Joint Duty Assignment Lists for consideration by senior decision makers.
- The results of this survey will not affect the joint duty status or credit of the incumbent of this position.

PRIVACY:

- Please do not put your name on the questionnaire. We will treat your answers as strictly private. We may combine your survey responses with other information about the Joint Duty Assignment List.
- Your supervisors and leaders will not be permitted to read your completed questionnaire, nor will we release any data that could possibly identify you by name or position to anyone in the Department of Defense or Federal Government, except as required by law. We will keep all hard copy and computer data files.
- The Deputy Secretary of Defense and the Chairman, Joint Chiefs of Staff, have endorsed this survey. Your first-hand input regarding the nature of the work required to be performed in the billet identified below is needed to assess the appropriateness of inclusion of this billet on the Joint Duty Assignment List.

IMPORTANT: This questionnaire is to be filled out by the person who is currently assigned to the billet/position listed at the right. If this person is not available to participate in the survey, then the SUPERVISOR of the billet/position or a qualified DESIGNATED INDIVIDUAL should complete this questionnaire and return it to your Survey Administrator. Please turn to page 2 for instructions for completing the questionnaire.

Thank you for participating in this important study!

INSTRUCTIONS - **Use #2 pencil only!**

1. **The survey is divided into two parts. Questions 1 - 21 request factual information about your current position and the work you do. These questions are mandatory. Questions 22 - 29 ask for voluntary opinions on selected topics. Although there is no penalty for not answering them, these questions are very important to the analysis of joint duty assignments.**
2. **Please answer EVERY question, UNLESS you are asked to skip a question that does not apply to you. If you're unsure about how to answer a question, obtain help from your organizational point of contact. Please give each question the best answer you can.**
3. **Answer the questions by:**
   - **MAKING HEAVY DARK MARKS** that fill the oval completely; **or by**
   - **WRITING IN** the answer, as requested.
4. **Some questions will ask you to provide estimates of the approximate amount of time you spend doing certain functions or working in an area or areas. Please look through the range of possible responses before writing in your response(s).**
5. **Please seal your completed questionnaire in the enclosed envelope and return it to the Survey Administrator at your location.**
6. **If you have any questions about the study, or have problems filling out your questionnaire, feel free to call the RAND-LMI survey director, Jennifer Hawes-Dawson collect at commercial:**

   (310) 393-0411, Extension 7238
7. **Please use the following definitions as you fill out your questionnaire.**

KEY DEFINITIONS

- **Military Department** refers to the Department of the Army, Department of the Navy, or Department of the Air Force.
- **Branch of Service or Service** refers to the United States Army, Navy, Air Force, Marine Corps, or Coast Guard and to the members of the armed forces of Allied nations.
- **Defense Agency** refers to organizations such as the Defense Logistics Agency, Defense Intelligence Agency, Defense Mapping Agency, Defense Information Systems Agency, On-site Inspection Agency, and others that provide defense-wide support and/or services.

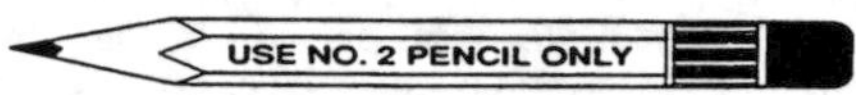

EVERYONE: To find out which questions apply to you please ANSWER Q. 1 below, and FOLLOW THE INSTRUCTION next to the answer you mark.

1. This questionnaire is being completed by:
   (Mark One Response)

   a. The person currently occupying the billet identified .... ① **Continue With Q. 2**

   b. The SUPERVISOR of the person occupying this billet .... ② GO TO Q. 10, ON PAGE 4

   c. ANOTHER PERSON designated to complete this survey .... ③ GO TO Q. 10, ON PAGE 4

REMINDER:

- **Complete questions 2 through 9 only if you are the person occupying the billet listed on the cover of this questionnaire.**
- **If you are a SUPERVISOR or ANOTHER PERSON designated to complete this questionnaire, go directly to question 10, on page 4.**

2. What is your **branch of Service?**
   (Mark One Response)

   a. US Army .... ①
   b. US Navy .... ②
   c. US Air Force .... ③
   d. US Marine Corps .... ④
   e. US Coast Guard .... ⑤

3. Who currently signs your official performance evaluation report (fitness report)?
   (Mark One Response in Each Row)

WHO IS YOUR:	US Army Officer	US Navy Officer	US Air Force Officer	US Marine Corps Officer	US Civilian	Allied Military	Not Appl.
a. Rater	①	②	③	④	⑤	⑥	⑦
b. Intermediate Rater or Reporting Senior	①	②	③	④	⑤	⑥	⑦
c. Senior Rater, Senior Reporting Officer or Reviewing Officer .	①	②	③	④	⑤	⑥	⑦

4. What is your present **pay grade**? **(Mark One Response)**

a. O1 .... ①
b. O2 .... ②
c. O3 .... ③
d. O4 .... ④
e. O5 .... ⑤
f. O6 .... ⑥
g. O7 to O10 .... ⑦

5. Please write in the number of **months** you have **served** in this billet.

Months

Write the number in the boxes. →

Then, fill the matching ovals below each box. →

⓪	⓪
①	①
②	②
③	③
④	④
⑤	⑤
⑥	⑥
⑦	⑦
⑧	⑧
⑨	⑨

6. Which of the following **military schools** which provide joint professional military education have you **completed**? **(Mark All That Apply)**

a. JPME Phase II (Armed Forces Staff College) .... ①
b. Army Command & General Staff College .... ②
c. Air Command & Staff College .... ③
d. Marine Corps Staff College .... ④
e. College of Naval Command & Staff (Naval War College) .... ⑤
f. Armed Forces Staff College (June 1990 and prior) ... ⑥
g. Foreign Intermediate Service College .... ⑦
h. Army War College .... ⑧
i. College of Naval Warfare (NWC) .... ⑨
j. Air War College .... ⑩
k. National War College .... ⑪
l. Industrial College of the Armed Forces .... ⑫
m. None of the above .... ⑬

NOTE: BEFORE ANSWERING QUESTIONS 7 - 9, PLEASE READ THE FOLLOWING INSTRUCTIONS

Army Officers:

Question 7: Enter your numeric Branch Code and Area of Concentration (AOC), e.g., 11A (Infantry). If you are single tracked in a functional area, enter your numeric functional area code and AOC in lieu of a branch code.

Question 8: Enter your functional area code and AOC here if you have one, e.g., 48F (Foreign Area Officer - China). If you have no functional area or you entered a functional area code and AOC in response to question 7 because you are single tracked in a functional area, please fill in code 9 for Not Applicable.

Question 9: Enter any Skill Identifier you have that is **relevant to your current duty assignment**, e.g., 6Z (Strategist) or 4Z (Certified Acquisition Officer). If you don't have a relevant Skill Identifier, please fill in code 9 for Not Applicable.

Navy Officers:

Question 7: Enter your numeric Designator, e.g., 1110 (Surface Warfare Officer.)

Question 8: Enter your Sub-specialty code, e.g., 54P (Naval/Mechanical Engineering). If you don't have a sub-specialty code, please fill in code 9 for Not Applicable.

Question 9: Enter your Additional Qualification Designator (AQD) that is **relevant to your current duty assignment,** e.g., APM (Fully qualified acquisition officer). If you don't have a relevant AQD, please fill in code 9 for Not Applicable. (Your most recent ODC may have the applicable data.)

Air Force Officers:

(Note: You may use the AFSCs that were in use prior to 1 October 1993 or if you know your new AFSC code, you can use it.)

Question 7: Enter your Primary AFSC, e.g., 1235N (Bomber Pilot), 1495 (Air Operations Officer-Pilot). The new AFSCs would be 11B2A (qualified pilot/co-pilot bomber) and 13B3 (qualified command & control operations officer).

Question 8: Enter your Secondary AFSC, e.g., 7016 (Executive Staff Officer), 5525 (Civil Engineer). The new AFSCs would be 37A3 (information management) and 32E3C (Civil Engineer). If you don't have a Secondary AFSC, please fill in code 9 for Not Applicable.

Air Force Officers (Continued):

Question 9: Enter your Tertiary AFSC, e.g., 7324 (Personnel Staff Officer), 6416 (Supply Management Officer). The new AFSCs would be 36P3 (personnel officer, qualified level) and 23S3 (supply officer, qualified level). If you don't have a Tertiary AFSC, please fill in code 9 for Not Applicable.

Marine Corps Officers:

Question 7: Enter your Primary Military Occupational Specialty (MOS), e.g., 0802 (Field Artillery Officer).

Question 8: Enter your Secondary MOS, e.g., 0402 (Logistics Officer). If you don't have a Secondary MOS, please fill in code 9 for Not Applicable.

Question 9: Enter your Tertiary MOS, e.g., 9650 (Operations Analyst). If you don't have a Tertiary MOS, please fill in code 9 for Not Applicable.

NOTE: BEFORE ANSWERING QUESTIONS 7 - 9, PLEASE READ INSTRUCTIONS ON PAGES 3 - 4.

7. Please write in **your primary** Military Specialty, Sub-Specialty, Designator, or AFSC.

Enter Code: ________

8. Please write in **your secondary or alternate** Military Specialty, Sub-Specialty, Designator, or AFSC.

Enter Code: ________

or, Mark here for Not Applicable ⑨

9. Please write in **your tertiary** Military Specialty, Sub-Specialty, Designator, or AFSC.

Enter Code: ________

or, Mark here for Not Applicable ⑨

Questions 10 - 18 refer to the billet listed on the cover of this questionnaire.

- **Please answer Q. 10 - Q. 18 about the duty requirements of the billet on the cover of this questionnaire.**

10. Pick the category which best characterizes the nature of the billet listed on the cover of the questionnaire. **(Mark One Response)**

a. Commander or Deputy Commander .... ①
b. Executive Assistant .... ②
c. Supervisor/leader of a staff element or operational team .... ③
d. Scientific or Technical Advisor .... ④
e. Staff Action Officer or Operational Watch Officer ..... ⑤
f. Administrative or Technical Support Staff Officer (ADP, LAN, Mil Sec, etc.) .... ⑥
g. Educator, trainer, or instructor .... ⑦
h. Other .... ⑧

If Code 8 for Other is filled in, please describe your billet below.

____

In the following questions, the term Military Department refers to the Department of the Army, Department of the Navy, or Department of the Air Force.

REMINDER: These questions refer to the person occupying the billet listed on the cover of the questionnaire.

11. Please answer "yes" or "no" to each of the following questions.

11a. Do you serve full-time with another **Military Department (e.g., an Air Force Officer assigned to a unit of the Army)** and are you formally assigned a billet in that **other Military Department**? (Such billets are called "Cross Department Positions".) **(Mark One Response)**

① Yes ② No

11b. Do you serve full-time with the **armed forces of another nation or with an international military or treaty organization (e.g., a US officer assigned to a billet in the headquarters of NATO; a liaison officer at the headquarters of a foreign military service; an officer assigned full-time to an element of the United Nations, etc.)** and are you formally assigned to a billet in that organization? **(Mark One Response)**

① Yes ② No

11c. Are you assigned to both your own **Military Department** and a **joint, combined, or international organization**? (Example, an officer assigned to a billet in the G3, Eighth US Army while simultaneously assigned to positions in the J3, US Forces Korea, and the C3, Combined Forces Command (ROK/US). (Such billets are referred to as "Dual Hat Positions".) **(Mark One Response)**

① Yes ② No

NOTE: In Questions 12 - 15 we ask you to report on the organizations you interact with, the areas you work in, and the functions you perform in those areas. We ask you to estimate the approximate percentage of time you spend on an **annual** basis working on matters involving exclusively your own Service or Organization, another or multiple Services, and other Nations.

Please use the following definitions as you fill out these questions.

- **EXCLUSIVELY YOUR OWN SERVICE OR ORGANIZATION** means you perform some duties concerning matters which pertain exclusively to your own Service or exclusively to the Organization to which you are assigned.

  Examples:

  An Army officer assigned to the Joint Staff who spends time making assessments of Army program submissions is working on matters pertaining exclusively to the Army.

  An Automation Support Officer assigned to a Unified Command Headquarters who is responsible for automation support in the Headquarters may be working on matters pertaining exclusively to the Unified Command.

- **ANOTHER OR MULTIPLE SERVICES** (one of which could be your own service) means you work on matters pertaining to a Service other than your own or you work on matters pertaining to multiple services.

- **OTHER NATIONS** means that you work on matters pertaining to other nations and their military forces.

Please look over the entire set of responses before you answer each question.

These questions refer to the billet listed on the cover of this questionnaire.

12. Indicate the **approximate percentage of time** you typically spend over the **course of one year** working with people OUTSIDE your organization assigned to each of the following organizations or types of organizations. **If you've been assigned to your billet less than one year, please provide your best estimate.**

    Please write in a response for each organization or type of organization you typically work with. The sum of your responses may be less than but not greater than 100%. (If a category does not apply to you, write "0" on the line.)

TIME TYPICALLY SPENT ANNUALLY WITH STAFF FROM OUTSIDE YOUR ORGANIZATION:	Approximate Percent of Time Spent
a. Other Nations	_______ %
b. Non-US Militaries or Governments	_______ %
c. Other Non-DoD US Departments or Agencies	_______ %
d. National Security Council	_______ %
e. The White House or Executive Office of the President	_______ %
f. Central Intelligence Agency	_______ %
g. Office of the Secretary of Defense	_______ %
h. One or more Defense Agencies	_______ %
i. One or more Unified or Specified Commands	_______ %
j. The Joint Staff	_______ %
k. US Army Activities	_______ %
l. US Navy Activities	_______ %
m. US Air Force Activities	_______ %
n. US Marine Corps Activities	_______ %
o. US Coast Guard Activities	_______ %
p. Other	_______ %

REMINDER:

The sum of your responses may be less than but not greater than 100%.

INSTRUCTIONS AND EXAMPLE FOR COMPLETING QUESTION 13

13. This question asks you to describe the primary duties and responsibilities of the billet identified on the cover page. Please read the following instructions and look over the completed example below before filling in your responses.

PART 1: Read the list of generic duties and responsibilities provided in categories a - k. Then fill in the code numbers for all categories that apply to your billet.

PART 2 (Shaded Column): For each primary duty that you filled in under part 1, please indicate the approximate percent of time you typically spend over the course of a year performing each of these duties. List the total time you typically spend on each duty. **The sum of the responses in the column marked part 2 should total 100%.**

PART 3: Under part 3, breakdown the total time estimate for each generic duty and responsibility entered in part 2 (shaded column). Indicate how much of this time was spent on matters involving exclusively your own Service or Organization, another or multiple Services, and other Nations. The sum of these times should equal the time entered in part 2 (shaded column).

PART 1 PRIMARY DUTIES: Be sure to fill in Part 2 and Part 3 for each category marked below → (Mark All That Apply)	PART 2 TOTAL TIME SPENT ON EACH DUTY =	PART 3 APPROXIMATE PERCENTAGE OF TIME SPENT ON MATTERS INVOLVING: Exclusively Your Own Service or Organization	+ Another or Multiple Service(s)	+ Other Nations
a. Exercising **operational command or operational control** of assigned combat or combat support forces 01	____ % =	____	+ ____	+ ____
b. Commanding, controlling, or directing **non-combat** units, organizations or activities 02	____ % =			
c. Conducting military **operations** (includes deploying forces, training exercises, unit training, etc.) 03	____ % =	**COMPLETED EXAMPLE FOR QUESTION 13**		
d. Providing **support to military operations** (includes intel, commo, logistics, etc.) 04	____ % =			
e. Providing **administrative or technical support** (includes ADP, admin support, contracting, education and other services, etc.) 05	____ % =	____	+ ____	+ ____
f. Developing, staffing, assessing, or implementing **plans** 06	____ % =	____	+ ____	+ ____
g. Developing, staffing or assessing **requirements** for forces and materiel ...... ●	40 % =	10	+ 30	+ 0
h. Developing, staffing or assessing **military doctrine** 08	____ % =	____	+ ____	+ ____
i. Developing, staffing or assessing **policies** .. ●	40 % =	0	+ 40	+ 0
j. Developing, staffing or assessing **program or budget submission(s)** .... ●	20 % =	10	+ 10	+ 0
k. Other .... 11 Please list the category below: ____	____ % =	____	+ ____	+ ____
	100%	**The sum of the responses should total 100%.**		

13. This question asks you to describe the primary duties and responsibilities of the billet identified on the cover page. Please read the instructions and look over the completed example on the opposite page (page 6) before filling in your responses. **Then answer this question about the identified billet.**

This is a complex question requiring careful attention. Please give your best estimate of the approximate amount of time spent on each area.

← **SEE INSTRUCTIONS AND EXAMPLE ON PAGE 6**

PART 1 PRIMARY DUTIES: Be sure to fill in Part 2 and Part 3 for each category filled in below → (Mark All That Apply)	PART 2 TOTAL TIME SPENT ON EACH DUTY =	PART 3 APPROXIMATE PERCENTAGE OF TIME SPENT ON MATTERS INVOLVING: Exclusively Your Own Service or Organization	+ Another or Multiple Service(s)	+ Other Nations
a. Exercising **operational command or operational control** of assigned combat or combat support forces 01	______ % =	______	+ ______	+ ______
b. Commanding, controlling, or directing **non-combat** units, organizations or activities 02	______ % =	______	+ ______	+ ______
c. Conducting military **operations** (includes deploying forces, training exercises, unit training, etc.) 03	______ % =	______	+ ______	+ ______
d. Providing **support to military operations** (includes intel, commo, logistics, etc.) 04	______ % =	______	+ ______	+ ______
e. Providing **administrative or technical support** (includes ADP, admin support, contracting, education and other services, etc.) 05	______ % =	______	+ ______	+ ______
f. Developing, staffing, assessing, or implementing **plans** 06	______ % =	______	+ ______	+ ______
g. Developing, staffing or assessing **requirements** for forces and materiel 07	______ % =	______	+ ______	+ ______
h. Developing, staffing or assessing **military doctrine** 08	______ % =	______	+ ______	+ ______
i. Developing, staffing or assessing **policies** .. 09	______ % =	______	+ ______	+ ______
j. Developing, staffing or assessing **program or budget submission(s)** 10	______ % =	______	+ ______	+ ______
k. Other.................................. 11 ↓ Please list the category below: ______________________	______ % =	______	+ ______	+ ______
	100%	**The sum of the responses should total 100%.**		

INSTRUCTIONS AND EXAMPLE FOR COMPLETING QUESTION 14

14. This question asks you to describe the principal areas or subject matters you typically work in over the course of a year. Please read the following instructions and look over the completed example below before filling in your responses. **Then answer this question about the person who occupies the billet on the cover of this questionnaire.**

PART 1: Read the list of principal areas or subject matters provided below. Then fill in the code numbers for all categories that apply to the billet identified on the cover of this questionnaire.

PART 2 (Shaded Column): For each principal area or subject matter you listed under part 1, please indicate the approximate percent of time you typically spend over the course of a year performing in that area or subject matter. List the **total** time you typically spend on each area. **The sum of the responses in the column marked part 2 should total 100%.**

PART 3: Under part 3, breakdown the total time estimate for each principal area/subject matter to indicate how much of this time was spent on matters involving exclusively your own Service or Organization, another or multiple Services, and other Nations. The sum of these times should equal the time entered in part 2 (shaded column).

PART 1 ENTER CODES FOR PRINCIPAL AREAS/SUBJECT MATTERS IN BOXES: Be sure to fill in Part 2 and Part 3 for each category filled in below →	PART 2 TOTAL TIME SPENT ON EACH DUTY =		PART 3 APPROXIMATE PERCENTAGE OF TIME SPENT ON MATTERS INVOLVING: Exclusively Your Own Service or Organization	+	Another or Multiple Service(s)	+	Other Nations
a. 01	10 %	=	5	+	5	+	0
b. 02	20 %	=	5	+	10	+	5
c. 04	40 %	=	10	+	30	+	0
d. 06	30 %	=	10	+	20	+	0
	100%						

COMPLETED EXAMPLE FOR QUESTION 14

LIST OF PRINCIPAL AREAS/SUBJECT MATTERS CODES FOR QUESTION 14. ENTER CODES IN BOXES FOR QUESTION 14, PART 1.

01 National Military Strategy & Policy Development (includes advice to President or NCA, CJCS, etc.)

02 Strategic Matters including Space and Operational Watch Standing (those designed to have a long-range effect on an enemy and his military forces/operations)

03 Mobilization

04 Force Development

05 Tactical Matters including Operational Watch Standing (those designed to have an immediate effect on an enemy and his military forces/operations, participation in training exercises, etc.)

06 Operations Other Than War including Operational Watch Standing (peacekeeping, humanitarian relief, CA/PSYOPS, disaster relief, counter-drug, etc.)

07 Special Operations (current OPS)

08 Intelligence

09 Communications

10 Medical/Health Services

11 Logistics (Supply, Maintenance, Transportation, etc.)

12 Mapping, Charting, Geodesy

13 Training (other than exercises)

14 Education & Professional Development

15 Resource Management or Financial Management

16 Engineering

17 Acquisition or Research & Development (includes Program/ Project Management or Coordination)

18 Contracting or Contract Management

19 Legal Affairs

20 Public Affairs

21 Automated data processing, information systems, software development, etc.

22 General Administration (includes general staff support, Aides, Executive Assistants, TQM, etc.)

23 Legislative Affairs

24 Scientific Matters (includes weather, environment, etc.)

25 Inspector General Activities

26 Manpower & Personnel

27 Politico-Military or Attache matters

28 Nuclear, Chemical or Biological

29 Law Enforcement, Physical Security or Investigations

30 Other
↓
Please write the area or subject below:

____

14. This question asks you to describe the principal areas or subject matters you typically work in over the course of a year. Please read the following instructions and look over the completed example on the opposite page (page 8) before filling in your responses. **Then answer this question about the person who occupies the identified billet.**

This is a complex question requiring careful attention. Please give your best estimate of the approximate amount of your time spent on each area.

← **SEE INSTRUCTIONS AND EXAMPLE ON PAGE 8**

PART 1 ENTER CODES FOR PRINCIPAL AREAS/SUBJECT MATTERS IN BOXES: Be sure to fill in Part 2 and Part 3 for each category filled in below → **Enter codes from the bottom of page 8 in the boxes below:**	PART 2 TOTAL TIME SPENT ON EACH DUTY =	PART 3 APPROXIMATE PERCENTAGE OF TIME SPENT ON MATTERS INVOLVING: Exclusively Your Own Service or Organization	+ Another or Multiple Service(s)	+ Other Nations
a. [|]	____ % =	____	+ ____	+ ____
b. [|]	____ % =	____	+ ____	+ ____
c. [|]	____ % =	____	+ ____	+ ____
d. [|]	____ % =	____	+ ____	+ ____
e. [|]	____ % =	____	+ ____	+ ____
f. [|]	____ % =	____	+ ____	+ ____
g. [|]	____ % =	____	+ ____	+ ____
h. [|]	____ % =	____	+ ____	+ ____
i. [|]	____ % =	____	+ ____	+ ____
j. [|]	____ % =	____	+ ____	+ ____
k. [|]	____ % =	____	+ ____	+ ____
l. [|]	____ % =	____	+ ____	+ ____
m. [|]	____ % =	____	+ ____	+ ____
Note: If you entered code 30 for OTHER, please write the area or subject below: ________________	100%	**The sum of the responses should total 100%.**		

INSTRUCTIONS FOR COMPLETING QUESTION 15

This question asks that you give the approximate percentage of the time you spend doing one or both of the tasks listed below.

- Read the two tasks listed in categories a and b. First indicate the total time you typically spend on each task over the course of a year. If you do not spend any time on that task, write "0" next to that item. Then breakdown the time estimate you listed to indicate how much of this time was spent on matters involving exclusively your own Service, another or multiple Services, and other Nations. The sum of the times should equal the time entered in the column marked total (shaded column). The sum of your responses does not have to total 100% but must not be greater than 100%.

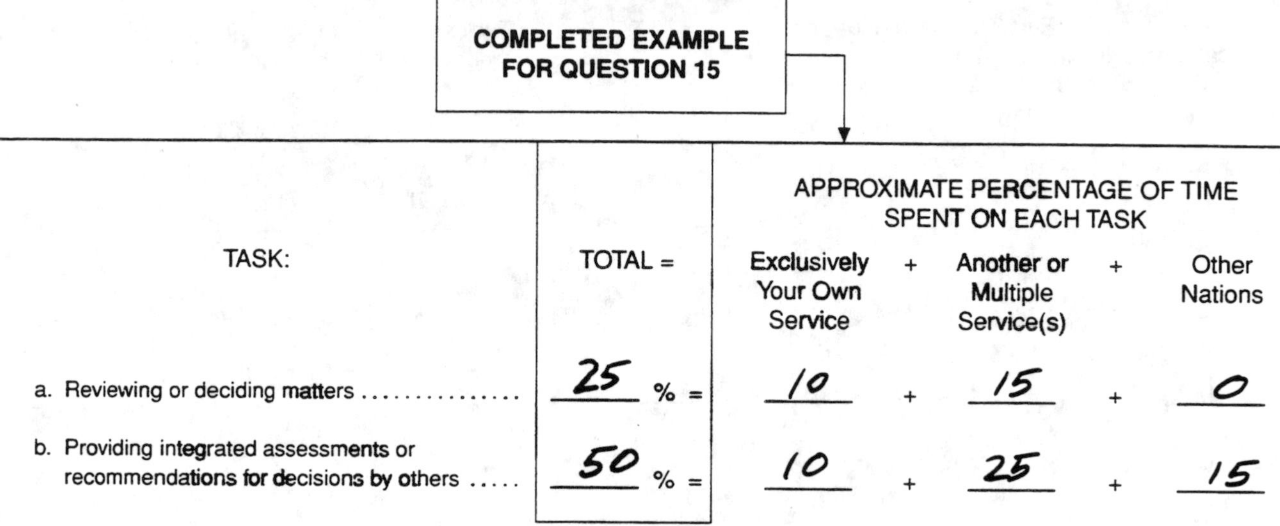

COMPLETED EXAMPLE FOR QUESTION 15

TASK:	TOTAL =		APPROXIMATE PERCENTAGE OF TIME SPENT ON EACH TASK				
			Exclusively Your Own Service	+	Another or Multiple Service(s)	+	Other Nations
a. Reviewing or deciding matters	25	% =	10	+	15	+	0
b. Providing integrated assessments or recommendations for decisions by others	50	% =	10	+	25	+	15

REMINDER: The sum of your responses may be less than 100% but may not exceed 100%.

EVERYONE, PLEASE ANSWER QUESTION 15 BELOW.
Question 15 refers to the person occupying the billet on the cover of the questionnaire.

15. Please indicate the **approximate percentage of the time** you spend doing one or both of the tasks listed. Please read the instructions and look at the completed example shown above before filling in your responses.

An example of how to complete this question is shown above.

TASK:	TOTAL =		APPROXIMATE PERCENTAGE OF TIME SPENT ON EACH TASK				
			Exclusively Your Own Service	+	Another or Multiple Service(s)	+	Other Nations
a. Reviewing or deciding matters	______	% =	______	+	______	+	______
b. Providing integrated assessments or recommendations for decisions by others	______	% =	______	+	______	+	______

REMINDER: The sum of your responses may be less than 100% but may not exceed 100%.

Questions 16 - 18 refer to the billet on the cover of the questionnaire.

16. Indicate which one of the following statements best describes the **primary focus of your efforts. (Mark One Response)**

a. The primary focus of my efforts is on operational or supportability matters pertaining to a CINC's Area of Responsibility (AOR) or several AORs .... ①

b. The primary focus of my efforts is on defense-wide issues or matters that affect one or more CINCs, Military Departments or Defense Agencies .... ②

17. Certain functions have been standardized among all Services, and in some cases, consolidated (e.g., finance). Do the duties or responsibilities of your billet require you to perform one or more **functions that have been standardized** throughout DoD? **(Mark One Response)**

a. Yes .... ①

b. No .... ②

c. Not sure .... ③

18. Please indicate which of the military services you interact with in the performance of your primary duties and responsibilities. Please fill in the numbers only for those services with whom you interact. **(Mark All That Apply)**

a. US Army .... ①

b. US Navy .... ②

c. US Air Force .... ③

d. US Marine Corps .... ④

e. US Coast Guard .... ⑤

Please indicate how much you agree or disagree with each of the following statements by marking the appropriate number in each row. Questions 19 - 21 refer to the billet on the cover of this questionnaire.

Strongly Disagree
Disagree
Neither Agree nor Disagree
Agree
Strongly Agree

19. Joint professional military education is essential to performing successfully in this billet .... ①②③④⑤

20. The person assigned to this billet should have prior knowledge of other services' or nations' military operations and capabilities gained through a prior joint duty assignment .. ①②③④⑤

21. The duties and responsibilities of this billet could be performed just as effectively by a civilian .... ①②③④⑤

Please continue on page 12 ⟶

NOTE:

- **Question 22 - 29 are voluntary opinion questions. See instructions on page 2.**
- **Complete questions 22 through 29 only if you are the person occupying the billet listed on the cover of this questionnaire.**
- **If you are a SUPERVISOR or ANOTHER PERSON designated to complete this questionnaire, this is the end of the survey. Read instructions at the bottom of this page.**

Please indicate how much you agree or disagree with each of the following statements by marking the appropriate number in each row.

Strongly Disagree
Disagree
Neither Agree nor Disagree
Agree
Strongly Agree

22. Joint duty assignments are highly sought after by career officers .... ① ② ③ ④ ⑤

23. It is difficult to fit a joint duty assignment in the normal career path of an officer like me .... ① ② ③ ④ ⑤

24. Officers serving in a joint duty assignment are not as competitive for promotion as their contemporaries in comparable service positions .... ① ② ③ ④ ⑤

Strongly Disagree
Disagree
Neither Agree nor Disagree
Agree
Strongly Agree

25. My position/responsibility could be performed by an officer of another service .... ① ② ③ ④ ⑤

26. My position/responsibility requires unique knowledge of my own service and could not be performed by an officer of another service .... ① ② ③ ④ ⑤

27. Morale problems will exist if joint duty credit is awarded for some positions in my immediate organization but not for others .... ① ② ③ ④ ⑤

28. I expect my present assignment to contribute significantly to my performance in my future service assignments .... ① ② ③ ④ ⑤

29. My Service's interest in assigning officers to joint duty assignments has increased .... ① ② ③ ④ ⑤

Thank you very much for participating in this survey. We would appreciate it if you'd seal your completed survey in the envelope provided and give it to the Survey Administrator at your location.

C. Detailed Results from the Group Sessions

This appendix presents the detailed results from group sessions that were designed to solicit views on different methodologies and criteria from senior decisionmakers.[1]

Background

The following three issues are associated with the use of a multi-criteria scoring methodology:

1. Which attributes or criteria to include in the methodology;
2. How much relative weight to place on each criterion;
3. How to generate scores for each criterion.

Our initial analysis indicated that five criteria might be useful for generating a joint score for each of the candidate billets. These criteria were Joint Time, Job Function, Number of Services, Organizational Context, and Grade. The score for Job Function was based on ten functional duties and twenty-nine subject matter areas.

We organized five group sessions with numerous defense officials to help address the three issues listed above. At each session, we asked the participants to provide relative weights on each of the five initial criteria and to provide relative values for each of the ten functional duties and twenty-nine subject matter areas. These sessions involved the following organizations:

1. Thirteen representatives from the J-1 directorates of the unified commands, the National Defense University, and several defense agencies.
2. General and flag officers from each of the services and the Joint Staff plus a senior civilian from the Office of the Secretary of Defense (Personnel and Readiness) that comprise the J-1's Executive Council for the report to Congress. There were seven participants in this session.

---

[1] The group sessions were conducted by the Logistics Management Institute.

3. Senior officers from seven of the Joint Staff directorates.
4. Senior officers from the personnel planning organizations of the four military services.
5. Ten officials from various defense agencies and organizations.

Relative Weights for Initial Criteria

At each session, the participants were led through a computer-assisted structured interview designed to elicit their opinions on the relative weights to place on each of the five initial criteria. The five criteria were presented in pairs and the respondent was asked for a relative value of one criterion against the other. The weights were derived using Saaty's Analytic Hierarchy Process.[2] Each participant provided his individual assessment of the appropriate weights; the sessions did not try to reach a consensus opinion. These weights represent how much each criterion should contribute to the measurement of the joint content of a billet. The results from the five group sessions are shown in Tables C.1 to C.5.

Table C.1

Relative Criteria Weights from J-1 Session

Participant	Joint Time	Job Function	Num. Services	Org. Context	Grade
1	0.25	0.43	0.14	0.11	0.07
2	0.19	0.32	0.06	0.36	0.07
3	0.49	0.12	0.23	0.07	0.09
4	0.36	0.39	0.07	0.14	0.04
5	0.19	0.33	0.18	0.20	0.10
6	0.37	0.30	0.11	0.16	0.06
7	0.38	0.31	0.19	0.07	0.05
8	0.33	0.25	0.25	0.12	0.05
9	0.40	0.33	0.14	0.07	0.06
10	0.48	0.25	0.14	0.08	0.05
11	0.32	0.39	0.09	0.15	0.05
12	0.44	0.26	0.13	0.12	0.05
13	0.24	0.32	0.24	0.14	0.06
Average	**0.34**	**0.31**	**0.15**	**0.14**	**0.06**
Std dev	**0.10**	**0.08**	**0.06**	**0.08**	**0.02**

[2]T. L. Saaty, *The Analytic Hierarchy Process*, McGraw-Hill, New York, 1980.

Table C.2

Relative Criteria Weights from Executive Council Session

Participant	Joint Time	Job Function	Num. Services	Org. Context	Grade
1	0.31	0.48	0.11	0.06	0.04
2	0.15	0.53	0.07	0.21	0.05
3	0.25	0.51	0.12	0.08	0.04
4	0.25	0.52	0.08	0.11	0.04
5	0.30	0.45	0.11	0.10	0.04
6	0.29	0.43	0.08	0.14	0.06
7	0.24	0.54	0.06	0.12	0.04
Average	**0.26**	**0.49**	**0.09**	**0.12**	**0.04**
Std dev	**0.05**	**0.04**	**0.02**	**0.05**	**0.01**

Table C.3

Relative Criteria Weights from Joint Staff Session

Participant	Joint Time	Job Function	Num. Services	Org. Context	Grade
1	0.46	0.25	0.08	0.15	0.06
2	0.26	0.46	0.14	0.10	0.04
3	0.17	0.44	0.21	0.13	0.05
4	0.30	0.35	0.20	0.10	0.05
5	0.33	0.42	0.14	0.08	0.03
6	0.47	0.27	0.08	0.13	0.05
7	0.18	0.52	0.10	0.13	0.07
Average	**0.31**	**0.39**	**0.14**	**0.12**	**0.05**
Std dev	**0.12**	**0.10**	**0.05**	**0.02**	**0.01**

Table C.4

Relative Criteria Weights from Personnel Planner Session

Participant	Joint Time	Job Function	Num. Services	Org. Context	Grade
1	0.58	0.23	0.04	0.10	0.05
2	0.50	0.15	0.23	0.08	0.04
3	0.26	0.44	0.09	0.16	0.05
4	0.18	0.20	0.47	0.09	0.06
Average	**0.38**	**0.26**	**0.21**	**0.11**	**0.05**
Std dev	**0.19**	**0.13**	**0.19**	**0.04**	**0.01**

The seven participants in the Executive Council session had very consistent responses (evidenced by low standard deviation). This is most likely due to their familiarity with the issues and their prior exposure to the candidate criteria and the results of the pilot survey analysis.

Table C.5

Relative Criteria Weights from Defense Agency Session

Participant	Joint Time	Job Function	Num. Services	Org. Context	Grade
1	0.49	0.14	0.22	0.10	0.05
2	0.27	0.13	0.45	0.10	0.05
3	0.25	0.46	0.14	0.09	0.06
4	0.28	0.47	0.15	0.07	0.03
5	0.26	0.47	0.08	0.15	0.04
6	0.33	0.43	0.07	0.12	0.05
7	0.21	0.53	0.08	0.13	0.05
8	0.43	0.17	0.28	0.07	0.05
9	0.29	0.46	0.13	0.08	0.04
10	0.16	0.42	0.05	0.29	0.08
Average	**0.30**	**0.37**	**0.17**	**0.12**	**0.05**
Std dev	**0.10**	**0.12**	**0.12**	**0.06**	**0.01**

The average weights for all the participants in the group sessions are shown in Table C.6.

The participants in the group sessions identified Joint Time and Job Function as the two most important criteria for measuring the joint content of a position. This was consistent with our reviews of the relevant literature and the categories used in the GAO study. The weights for the other three criteria were all fairly low. Furthermore, we felt that determining scores for the Organizational Context and Grade criteria would be highly subjective. For all these reasons, we felt it was important to understand the relative weights participants in the group sessions would place on the Joint Time and Job Function criteria alone.

The literature reviews, interviews, and GAO study suggested that Job Function needed further definition on what a person did when working on matters involving multiple services or other nations and what a person did when working on matters involving his own service or organization. We, therefore,

Table C.6

Average Criteria Weights from Group Sessions

Criterion	Average Weight
Joint Time	0.32
Job Function	0.36
Num. Services	0.15
Org. Context	0.12
Grade	0.05

split the Job Function criterion into Joint Function and Nonjoint Function. Again, we were interested in how the group participants would weight these two aspects of a position's duties and responsibilities.

During the last two group sessions (those involving the service personnel planners and the defense agencies), we posed these issues to the participants using a pencil-and-paper exercise. The results are shown in Table C.7.

The participants in these last two group sessions suggested Joint Time and Job Function should have approximately equal weights. This was consistent with the initial weights placed on these criteria when all five criteria were evaluated. Furthermore, the participants suggested that Joint Function should have twice the weight as Nonjoint Function. These findings were used to determine the weights for the criteria in our various multi-criteria algorithms.

Relative Values for Functional Duties and Subject Areas

The scores for the Joint and Nonjoint Function criteria are based on a combination of the duties a person performs and the subject areas addressed. Ten functional duties and twenty-nine subject areas were listed as options in the survey questionnaire. Respondents distributed their time across the ten functional duties, distinguishing the time spent on matters involving their own service or organization, multiple services, and other nations. They provided the same distribution of time across the twenty-nine subject areas.

Table C.7

Calculation of Revised Weights

Participant	Joint Time	Job Function	Joint Function	Nonjoint Function
1	0.57	0.43	0.60	0.40
2	0.20	0.80	0.67	0.33
3	0.67	0.33	0.75	0.25
4	0.83	0.17	0.83	0.17
5	0.33	0.67	0.50	0.50
6	0.33	0.67	0.50	0.50
7	0.60	0.40	0.55	0.45
8	0.40	0.60	0.50	0.50
9	0.67	0.33	0.50	0.50
10	0.33	0.67	0.67	0.33
11	0.33	0.67	0.75	0.25
12	0.20	0.80	0.67	0.33
13	0.20	0.80	0.60	0.40
14	0.67	0.33	0.75	0.25
Average	**0.46**	**0.54**	**0.63**	**0.37**
Std dev	**0.20**	**0.20**	**0.11**	**0.11**

To calculate scores for the responses, we needed relative values for the different duties and areas. This issue was presented to the participants of the last four group sessions, where the participants interacted with a software program designed to elicit their impressions of the relative weights of the different options. The resulting values from the four group sessions for the ten different functional duties are shown in Tables C.8 to C.11.

Table C.8

Duty Values from Executive Council Session

	Respondent							
Duty	1	2	3	4	5	6	7	Average
Command & control	10.00	10.00	10.00	10.00	10.00	10.00	10.00	10.00
Planning	10.00	6.00	9.38	9.33	8.82	10.00	5.91	8.49
Conduct milops	6.67	9.00	8.75	10.00	8.82	9.44	8.64	8.76
Noncombat C&C	10.00	8.00	5.63	6.67	7.65	6.67	6.82	7.35
Support to milops	10.00	7.00	8.13	6.67	7.65	6.67	5.91	7.43
Policy	6.67	1.00	6.88	6.00	5.88	5.56	0.00	4.57
Doctrine	5.66	4.00	4.38	5.33	7.06	1.67	0.00	4.01
Requirements	6.67	3.00	4.38	6.67	1.18	3.33	1.82	3.86
Program/ budget	0.67	1.50	2.50	4.67	1.18	1.67	0.00	1.74
Admin/ tech spt	0.67	0.50	2.50	1.33	0.59	0.56	6.36	1.79

Table C.9

Duty Values from Joint Staff Session

	Respondent							
Duty	1	2	3	4	5	6	7	Average
Command & control	10.00	10.00	10.00	8.00	10.00	10.00	9.47	9.64
Planning	6.25	6.00	3.64	6.00	7.50	7.50	6.31	6.17
Conduct milops	9.38	8.00	6.82	10.00	9.00	7.50	10.00	8.67
Noncombat C&C	8.75	5.20	4.55	5.00	7.50	6.88	7.37	6.46
Support to milops	6.87	4.00	4.55	6.00	5.00	7.50	5.79	5.67
Policy	3.13	1.20	3.18	4.00	2.50	5.00	2.63	3.09
Doctrine	4.37	2.40	3.64	4.00	4.00	5.00	2.63	3.72
Requirements	5.00	1.20	3.64	2.50	2.00	5.00	4.21	3.36
Program/ budget	3.75	1.60	3.18	2.50	1.00	5.00	3.68	2.96
Admin/ tech spt	2.50	0.40	2.27	2.00	1.50	3.13	1.58	1.91

Table C.10

Duty Values from Service Personnel Planner Session

Duty	Respondent 1	2	3	4	Average
Command & control	10.00	10.00	10.00	10.00	10.00
Planning	10.00	7.50	7.50	8.00	8.25
Conduct milops	10.00	7.50	5.00	10.00	8.13
Noncombat C&C	10.00	2.50	5.00	6.67	6.04
Support to milops	10.00	2.50	5.00	3.33	5.21
Policy	10.00	7.50	7.50	8.00	8.25
Doctrine	10.00	5.00	2.50	7.33	6.21
Requirements	10.00	2.50	2.50	6.67	5.42
Program/budget	10.00	2.50	2.50	3.33	4.58
Admin/tech spt	10.00	2.50	2.50	3.33	4.58

The average values and standard deviations from each group session are shown in Table C.12. The overall weighted average is shown along with the "normalized" average. The average for each group was normalized to a high score of ten. That is, if the highest average value was a 8.0, then all values were multiplied by 1.25 (8 divided by 10). This normalization was necessary because we wanted all criteria scores to be on a 0 to 10 basis.

We rounded the normalized values in Table C.12 to the nearest integer and used the rounded values for functional duties to calculate the Joint and Nonjoint Function scores. These ultimate duty values are shown in Table 2.2 in the body of the report.

A similar process was used to elicit values from the group participants for the twenty-nine subject areas. The average values for each of the four groups plus the overall weighted average and the normalized average are shown in Table C.13. The normalized values were rounded to the nearest one-half (e.g., 7.69 was rounded to 7.5) and used to calculate the score for the Joint and Nonjoint Function criteria. These ultimate subject area scores are shown in Table 2.3 in the body of the report.

Table C.11

Duty Values from Defense Agency Session

Duty	Respondent										Average
	1	2	3	4	5	6	7	8	9	10	
Command & control	8.94	4.67	7.50	10.00	18.89	10.00	9.41	9.33	10.00	7.06	8.58
Planning	4.25	8.67	8.75	7.37	10.00	6.84	6.47	8.00	6.00	5.29	7.16
Conduct milops	10.00	4.00	10.00	8.95	8.33	9.47	10.00	10.00	10.00	10.00	9.08
Noncombat C&C	7.24	6.67	3.75	2.11	2.78	1.58	3.53	5.33	1.50	4.71	3.92
Support to milops	7.45	6.67	6.88	9.47	5.56	7.89	9.41	8.00	7.50	5.88	7.47
Policy	3.19	10.00	5.00	0.53	3.89	2.11	2.35	5.33	2.00	4.71	3.91
Doctrine	1.28	9.33	8.75	4.21	7.22	2.63	5.88	5.33	6.00	5.29	5.59
Requirements	9.57	8.00	7.50	4.74	7.78	9.47	7.06	8.67	4.00	5.88	7.27
Program/budget	2.98	5.33	3.75	4.74	0.56	2.11	2.94	6.00	2.50	5.29	3.62
Admin/tech spt	1.06	3.33	0.63	0.53	0.56	0.53	1.76	0.67	0.50	4.71	1.43

Table C.12

Average Duty Values

Duty	Exec Council	Joint Staff	Svc Planners	Defense Agencies	Weighted	Normalized
	Avg/Std Dev	Avg/Std Dev	Avg/Std Dev	Avg/Std Dev	Average	Average
Command & control	10.00/0.00	9.64/0.75	10.00/0.00	8.58/1.71	9.40	10.00
Planning	8.49/1.78	6.17/1.29	8.25/1.19	7.16/1.75	7.40	7.88
Conduct milops	8.76/1.04	8.67/1.25	8.13/2.39	9.08/1.87	8.76	9.32
Noncombat C&C	7.35/1.40	6.46/1.57	6.04/3.15	3.92/2.04	5.72	6.08
Support to milops	7.43/1.34	5.67/1.25	5.21/3.36	7.47/1.31	6.69	7.12
Policy	4.57/2.83	3.09/1.20	8.25/1.19	3.91/2.63	4.49	4.78
Doctrine	4.01/2.43	3.72/0.93	6.21/3.21	5.59/2.50	4.82	5.13
Requirements	3.86/2.18	3.36/1.50	5.42/3.63	7.27/1.89	5.18	5.51
Program/budget	1.74/1.51	2.96/1.37	4.58/3.63	3.62/1.71	3.12	3.32
Admin/tech spt	1.79/2.14	1.91/0.87	4.58/3.63	1.43/1.46	2.09	2.22

Table C.13

Subject Area Values from Group Sessions

Subject Area	Executive Council Average	Joint Staff Average	Service Planners Average	Defense Agencies Average	Weighted Average	Normalized Average
Strategic matters	10.00	8.71	10.00	7.94	8.98	9.13
Nat mil strategy	9.76	10.00	9.23	10.00	9.83	10.00
Ops other than war	7.95	7.80	8.35	6.76	7.56	7.69
Logistics	7.83	7.40	6.74	8.13	7.68	7.81
Tactical matters	7.71	8.99	9.44	6.79	7.94	8.08
Special operations	7.59	8.11	8.34	8.26	8.05	8.19
Intelligence	7.23	6.43	6.89	8.05	7.27	7.40
Communications	6.99	6.77	6.55	7.67	7.11	7.23
Mobilization	6.75	5.83	7.61	5.95	6.37	6.48
Force development	6.75	8.40	7.13	7.48	7.45	7.58
Pol-mil/attache'	4.22	3.61	6.43	3.76	4.22	4.29
Training	3.61	7.59	6.21	4.12	5.11	5.19
Educ/prof develop	3.25	3.63	5.08	3.34	3.63	3.69
Nuc, bio, chem	3.01	6.67	6.93	5.18	5.18	5.27
Manpower & personnel	2.77	5.37	4.42	3.38	3.84	3.90
Medical/health svcs	2.65	5.12	3.66	3.18	3.57	3.63
Map, chart, geodesy	2.65	4.19	3.96	4.39	3.80	3.87
Scientific matters	2.41	3.14	4.41	3.86	3.36	3.42
ADP/info systems	2.29	3.56	3.43	4.99	3.68	3.75
Acquisition/R&D	2.17	4.46	4.84	5.54	4.25	4.33

Table C.13—continued

Subject Area	Executive Council Average	Joint Staff Average	Service Planners Average	Defense Agencies Average	Weighted Average	Normalized Average
Resource/fin mgmt	1.69	3.99	3.24	3.56	3.10	3.16
General admin	1.57	1.69	2.25	1.10	1.53	1.56
Legislative affairs	1.57	2.48	2.28	0.95	1.67	1.70
Engineering	1.45	3.68	3.36	4.35	3.25	3.31
Public affairs	1.45	2.56	2.16	1.43	1.81	1.84
Contracts/cont mgmt	1.33	2.50	2.93	3.44	2.56	2.60
Legal affairs	1.33	2.48	2.16	0.95	1.59	1.62
Law enforcement	1.20	1.73	2.99	1.69	1.74	1.77
IG activities	1.08	1.30	2.36	1.12	1.32	1.35

D. Results of Responses to the Survey's Opinion Questions

The survey sent to all candidate positions gathered three types of data. Questions 1 through 11 addressed the attributes of the person filling the position, including grade, service, and skill designations. Questions 12 through 18 asked about the duties and responsibilities of the position, including the amount of time spent working on matters involving multiple services or other nations. Finally, questions 19 through 29 solicited various opinions from the respondents about joint duty assignments. This appendix presents summary statistics on the responses to the opinion questions.

The survey respondents were asked to indicate how much they agreed or disagreed with specific questions by indicating one of the following five responses—strongly agree, agree, neither disagree nor agree, disagree, strongly disagree. For each of the opinion questions, the tables in this appendix summarize the responses in several ways—by grade, by service, by selected DoD occupational skill group, by organizational group, and by whether the respondent is currently on the Joint Duty Assignment List or not.[1] Some small cells are not shown separately in the data but are included in the All responses total.

Figure D.1 summarizes the responses to the opinion questions. This figure aggregates the "strongly agree/agree" and "disagree/strongly disagree" responses and orders the questions by the greatest differences between the two. The tables that follow (D.1–D.39) give more detail about each question and show responses by grade, service, organization, and occupation.

In general, the vast majority of respondents perceived that the billets were fungible across services, that is, that an officer of one service could perform the position/responsibility as well as an officer of another service (Q25). This opinion has import in deciding how to allocate billets across services.

[1]The grade, service, and functional skill are the requirements placed on the billet. These may not match the grade, service, and functional skill of the respondent.

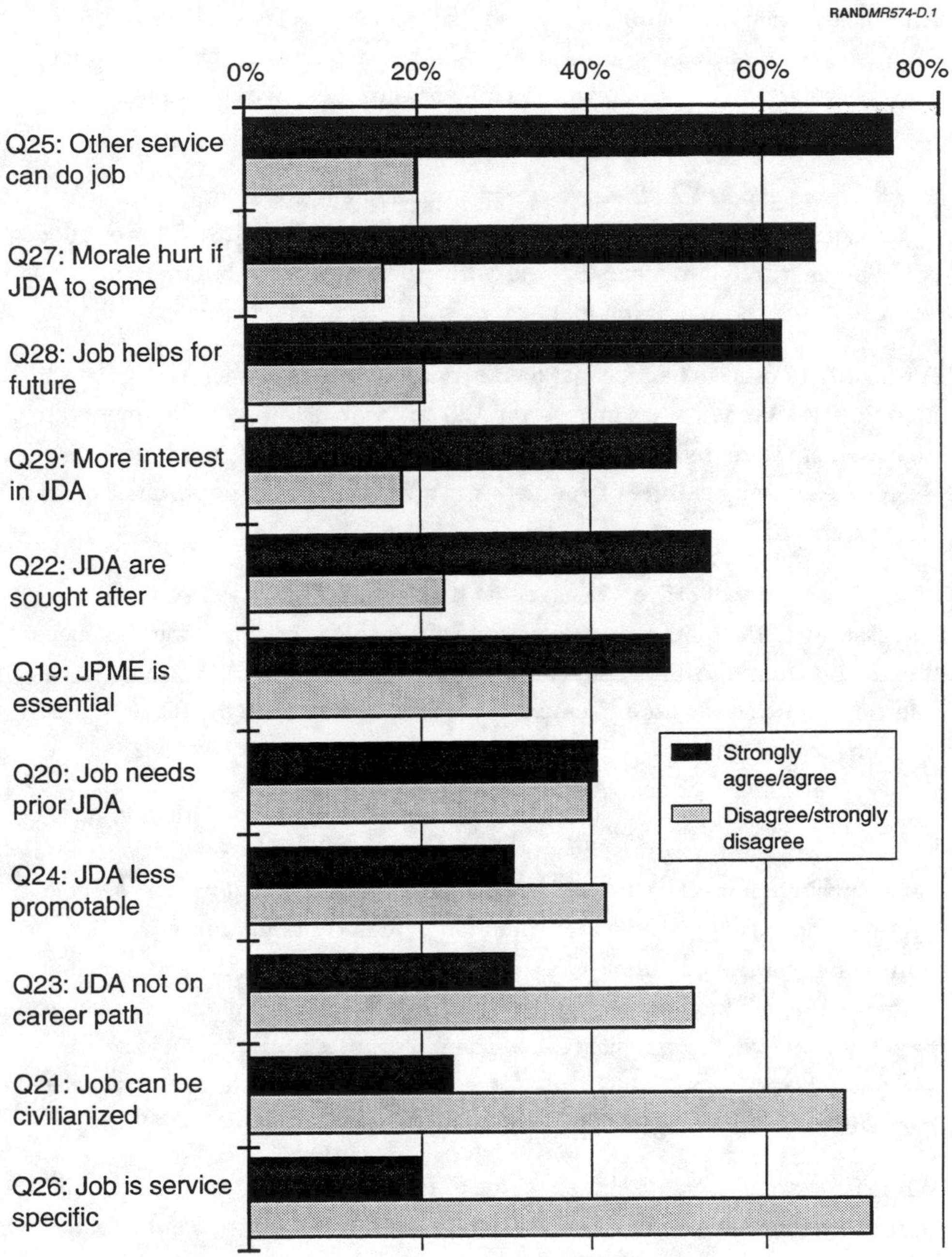

RANDMR574-D.1

0%
20%
40%
60%
80%
Q25: Other service can do job
Q27: Morale hurt if JDA to some
Q28: Job helps for future
Q29: More interest in JDA
Q22: JDA are sought after
Q19: JPME is essential
Q20: Job needs prior JDA
Q24: JDA less promotable
Q23: JDA not on career path
Q21: Job can be civilianized
Q26: Job is service specific
Strongly agree/agree
Disagree/strongly disagree

Figure D.1—Summary of Responses to Opinion Questions

Also, a large majority of officers agreed that morale problems will exist if joint duty credit is awarded for some positions in an immediate organization but not for others (Q27). This opinion affects how organizations would implement a JDAL.

Most officers expect that their service in a candidate JDAL billet will contribute significantly to performance in future service assignments (Q28). This opinion could be interpreted to mean that the culture of jointness has begun to take hold because it reflects an opinion that "jointness" matters even in service careers.

A majority of officers believe that their service's interest in assigning officers to joint duty assignments has increased (Q29) and that joint duty assignments are highly sought after by career officers (Q22). These responses also appear to reflect the growing culture of jointness and awareness of the importance of such assignments to careers.

Nearly a majority of officers believe that JPME is essential to performing successfully in the billet than the opposite (Q19). Slightly more officers believe that the officer in the billet should have had a prior JDA (Q20). For both questions, much stronger agreement exists for billets now on the JDAL. These opinions are useful in assessing criticality of positions in that JSOs are expected to have JPME and a prior JDA before filling a critical billet.

The next two questions must be interpreted carefully because the "disagrees" have a positive impact. More officers disagree than agree that officers serving in a JDA are not as competitive for promotion as their contemporaries in comparable service positions (Q24). Additionally, more officers, and a majority of them, disagree than agree that it is difficult to fit a JDA in the normal career path than believe the opposite (Q23). These responses indicate that joint assignments can be made to fit into career paths, and that officers do not believe they will be disadvantaged in promotion by such assignments.

While far more officers disagree that the duties and responsibilities of the billet could be performed just as effectively by a civilian, nearly 25 percent of officers agree with this statement (Q25).

Finally, over 70 percent of respondents disagree that the position/responsibility requires unique knowledge of one service and could not be performed by an officer of another service (Q26). This is a mirror image of the first question in the figure (Q25) and also illustrates the general fungibility of billets across services.

Question 19: joint professional military education is essential to performing successfully in this billet.

Table D.1

Question 19: Responses by Grade

GRADE	OPINION OF THOSE WHO ANSWERED					NO ANSWER
	Strongly Agree	Agree	Neither Agree/Disagree	Disagree	Strongly Disagree	
O-3	7%	23%	23%	32%	14%	1%
O-4	16%	30%	19%	22%	13%	0%
O-5	21%	34%	16%	19%	10%	0%
O-6	26%	35%	16%	17%	6%	1%
O-7+	20%	41%	17%	16%	5%	0%
All	18%	31%	18%	22%	11%	0%

Table D.2

Question 19: Responses by Type Organization

ORGANIZATION	OPINION OF THOSE WHO ANSWERED					NO ANSWER
	Strongly Agree	Agree	Neither Agree/Disagree	Disagree	Strongly Disagree	
Joint Staff	22%	37%	15%	17%	9%	0%
Warfighting CINCs	20%	31%	18%	21%	10%	0%
Supporting CINCs	14%	30%	17%	25%	14%	1%
WHS/OSD	18%	34%	17%	19%	12%	0%
Defense agencies	15%	29%	20%	24%	12%	1%
In-service	24%	35%	21%	16%	5%	1%
All others	18%	30%	17%	24%	11%	0%
All responses	18%	31%	18%	22%	11%	0%

Table D.3

Question 19: Responses by Skill Group

SKILL GROUP	OPINION OF THOSE WHO ANSWERED					NO ANSWER
	Strongly Agree	Agree	Neither Agree/Disagree	Disagree	Strongly Disagree	
Tactical operations	21%	32%	16%	21%	11%	0%
Intelligence	17%	30%	19%	22%	12%	1%
Engineer/maintenance	15%	30%	20%	24%	11%	0%
Scientists/profession	18%	32%	19%	20%	12%	0%
Supply/procure/allied	17%	31%	19%	22%	10%	1%
Administration	14%	29%	20%	26%	11%	1%
All responses	18%	31%	18%	22%	11%	0%

Table D.4

Question 19: Responses by Current Joint Assignment

POSITION	OPINION OF THOSE WHO ANSWERED					NO ANSWER
	Strongly Agree	Agree	Neither Agree/Disagree	Disagree	Strongly Disagree	
On current JDAL	21%	34%	16%	19%	10%	0%
Not on JDAL	12%	27%	22%	27%	12%	1%
All responses	17%	31%	18%	22%	11%	0%

Question 20: the person assigned to this billet should have prior knowledge of other services' or nations' military operations and capabilities gained through a prior joint duty assignment.

Table D.5

Question 20: Responses by Grade

GRADE	OPINION OF THOSE WHO ANSWERED					NO ANSWER
	Strongly Agree	Agree	Neither Agree/Disagree	Disagree	Strongly Disagree	
O-3	5%	19%	21%	39%	16%	1%
O-4	11%	24%	20%	33%	12%	0%
O-5	17%	27%	20%	26%	9%	0%
O-6	26%	33%	16%	20%	6%	1%
O-7+	29%	37%	14%	15%	5%	0%
All	18%	26%	19%	30%	10%	1%

Table D.6

Question 20: Responses by Type Organization

ORGANIZATION	OPINION OF THOSE WHO ANSWERED					NO ANSWER
	Strongly Agree	Agree	Neither Agree/Disagree	Disagree	Strongly Disagree	
Joint Staff	14%	24%	22%	29%	12%	0%
Warfighting CINCs	17%	28%	18%	28%	8%	0%
Supporting CINCs	10%	23%	19%	35%	14%	1%
WHS/OSD	15%	30%	22%	23%	11%	0%
Defense agencies	12%	25%	20%	31%	11%	1%
In-service	20%	35%	19%	21%	5%	1%
All others	18%	23%	19%	30%	10%	0%
All responses	15%	26%	19%	30%	10%	1%

Table D.7

Question 20: Responses by Skill Group

SKILL GROUP	OPINION OF THOSE WHO ANSWERED					NO ANSWER
	Strongly Agree	Agree	Neither Agree/Disagree	Disagree	Strongly Disagree	
Tactical operations	16%	25%	18%	30%	11%	0%
Intelligence	17%	31%	19%	25%	8%	1%
Engineer/maintenance	11%	25%	19%	33%	12%	1%
Scientists/profession	18%	25%	19%	30%	8%	0%
Supply/procure/allied	13%	24%	22%	30%	11%	1%
Administration	10%	24%	21%	33%	12%	1%
All responses	15%	26%	19%	30%	10%	1%

Table D.8

Question 20: Responses by Current Joint Assignment

POSITION	OPINION OF THOSE WHO ANSWERED					NO ANSWER
	Strongly Agree	Agree	Neither Agree/Disagree	Disagree	Strongly Disagree	
On current JDAL	18%	27%	19%	28%	9%	0%
Not on JDAL	10%	24%	20%	33%	12%	1%
All responses	15%	26%	19%	30%	10%	1%

Question 21: the duties and responsibilities of this billet could be performed just as effectively by a civilian.

Table D.9

Question 21: Responses by Grade

GRADE	OPINION OF THOSE WHO ANSWERED					NO ANSWER
	Strongly Agree	Agree	Neither Agree/Disagree	Disagree	Strongly Disagree	
O-3	16%	23%	10%	22%	29%	1%
O-4	10%	16%	8%	25%	41%	0%
O-5	7%	12%	8%	25%	47%	0%
O-6	5%	8%	5%	22%	61%	1%
O-7+	3%	6%	3%	14%	74%	0%
All	9%	15%	8%	24%	44%	0%

Table D.10

Question 21: Responses by Type Organization

ORGANIZATION	OPINION OF THOSE WHO ANSWERED					NO ANSWER
	Strongly Agree	Agree	Neither Agree/Disagree	Disagree	Strongly Disagree	
Joint Staff	6%	9%	6%	21%	59%	0%
Warfighting CINCs	7%	12%	6%	24%	51%	0%
Supporting CINCs	10%	18%	8%	24%	40%	1%
WHS/OSD	7%	14%	6%	28%	45%	1%
Defense agencies	14%	20%	11%	25%	30%	1%
In-service	3%	6%	5%	21%	66%	0%
All others	7%	11%	6%	24%	52%	0%
All responses	9%	15%	8%	24%	44%	0%

Table D.11

Question 21: Responses by Skill Group

SKILL GROUP	OPINION OF THOSE WHO ANSWERED					NO ANSWER
	Strongly Agree	Agree	Neither Agree/Disagree	Disagree	Strongly Disagree	
Tactical operations	5%	8%	5%	21%	61%	0%
Intelligence	11%	17%	11%	26%	36%	1%
Engineer/maintenance	13%	23%	9%	3%	32%	0%
Scientists/profession	8%	5%	9%	26%	42%	0%
Supply/procure/allied	9%	15%	8%	26%	41%	1%
Administration	12%	18%	8%	27%	36%	1%
All responses	9%	15%	8%	24%	44%	0%

Question 22: joint duty assignments are highly sought after by career officers.

Table D.12

Question 22: Responses by Grade

GRADE	OPINION OF THOSE WHO ANSWERED					NO ANSWER
	Strongly Agree	Agree	Neither Agree/Disagree	Disagree	Strongly Disagree	
O-3	23%	40%	24%	11%	3%	20%
O-4	17%	38%	24%	16%	5%	15%
O-5	13%	37%	23%	21%	6%	11%
O-6	14%	41%	19%	20%	6%	8%
O-7+	17%	43%	24%	15%	2%	17%
All	16%	38%	23%	18%	5%	24%

Table D.13

Question 22: Responses by Service

SERVICE	OPINION OF THOSE WHO ANSWERED					NO ANSWER
	Strongly Agree	Agree	Neither Agree/Disagree	Disagree	Strongly Disagree	
Army	12%	34%	25%	22%	7%	14%
Navy	17%	36%	22%	19%	6%	12%
Air Force	18%	43%	22%	14%	3%	13%
Marine Corps	15%	36%	28%	16%	6%	14%
All responses	16%	38%	23%	18%	5%	14%

Table D.14

Question 22: Responses by Skill

SKILL GROUP	OPINION OF THOSE WHO ANSWERED					NO ANSWER
	Strongly Agree	Agree	Neither Agree/Disagree	Disagree	Strongly Disagree	
Tactical operations	16%	41%	22%	17%	5%	11%
Intelligence	15%	37%	24%	18%	6%	18%
Engineer/maintenance	18%	38%	24%	15%	4%	19%
Scientists/profession	11%	36%	25%	22%	6%	13%
Supply/procure/allied	16%	40%	22%	17%	4%	10%
Administration	19%	36%	21%	19%	5%	12%
All responses	16%	38%	23%	18%	5%	14%

Table D.15

Question 22: Responses by Current Joint Assignment

POSITION	OPINION OF THOSE WHO ANSWERED					NO ANSWER
	Strongly Agree	Agree	Neither Agree/Disagree	Disagree	Strongly Disagree	
On current JDAL	13%	38%	23%	20%	6%	10%
Not on JDAL	20%	39%	23%	13%	4%	18%
All responses	16%	38%	23%	18%	5%	14%

Question 23: it is difficult to fit a joint duty assignment in the normal career path of an officer like me.

Table D.16

Question 23: Responses by Grade

GRADE	OPINION OF THOSE WHO ANSWERED					NO ANSWER
	Strongly Agree	Agree	Neither Agree/Disagree	Disagree	Strongly Disagree	
O-3	7%	20%	23%	40%	10%	20%
O-4	9%	21%	17%	43%	10%	15%
O-5	10%	22%	16%	41%	11%	11%
O-6	10%	24%	13%	39%	14%	8%
O-7+	8%	29%	13%	38%	12%	17%
All	9%	22%	17%	41%	11%	14%

Table D.17

Question 23: Responses by Service

SERVICE	OPINION OF THOSE WHO ANSWERED					NO ANSWER
	Strongly Agree	Agree	Neither Agree/Disagree	Disagree	Strongly Disagree	
Army	9%	22%	17%	41%	10%	15%
Navy	14%	25%	15%	36%	10%	12%
Air Force	6%	19%	18%	44%	13%	13%
Marine Corps	10%	25%	17%	41%	8%	14%
All responses	9%	22%	17%	41%	11%	14%

Table D.18

Question 23: Responses by Skill Group

SKILL GROUP	OPINION OF THOSE WHO ANSWERED					NO ANSWER
	Strongly Agree	Agree	Neither Agree/Disagree	Disagree	Strongly Disagree	
Tactical operations	9%	26%	17%	38%	9%	11%
Intelligence	6%	13%	18%	47%	17%	18%
Engineer/maintenance	7%	20%	19%	44%	11%	19%
Scientists/profession	9%	22%	16%	42%	11%	13%
Supply/procure/allied	11%	23%	16%	40%	11%	10%
Administration	10%	22%	17%	42%	10%	12%
All responses	9%	22%	17%	41%	11%	14%

Table D.19

Question 23: Responses by Current Joint Assignment

POSITION	OPINION OF THOSE WHO ANSWERED					NO ANSWER
	Strongly Agree	Agree	Neither Agree/Disagree	Disagree	Strongly Disagree	
On current JDAL	10%	22%	20%	38%	10%	10%
Not on JDAL	20%	39%	23%	13%	4%	18%
All responses	9%	22%	17%	41%	11%	14%

Question 24: officers serving in a joint duty assignment are not as competitive for promotion as their contemporaries in comparable service positions.

Table D.20

Question 24: Responses by Grade

GRADE	OPINION OF THOSE WHO ANSWERED					NO ANSWER
	Strongly Agree	Agree	Neither Agree/Disagree	Disagree	Strongly Disagree	
O-3	9%	15%	35%	33%	9%	20%
O-4	12%	19%	29%	32%	9%	15%
O-5	15%	21%	24%	31%	9%	11%
O-6	12%	20%	19%	38%	11%	8%
O-7+	5%	13%	19%	46%	17%	17%
All	12%	19%	26%	33%	9%	14%

Table D.21

Question 24: Responses by Service

SERVICE	OPINION OF THOSE WHO ANSWERED					NO ANSWER
	Strongly Agree	Agree	Neither Agree/Disagree	Disagree	Strongly Disagree	
Army	14%	21%	26%	30%	8%	15%
Navy	15%	19%	25%	31%	10%	13%
Air Force	9%	17%	27%	37%	10%	13%
Marine Corps	17%	20%	28%	26%	10%	14%
All responses	12%	19%	26%	33%	9%	14%

Table D.22

Question 24: Responses by Skill Group

SKILL GROUP	OPINION OF THOSE WHO ANSWERED					NO ANSWER
	Strongly Agree	Agree	Neither Agree/Disagree	Disagree	Strongly Disagree	
Tactical operations	13%	19%	25%	34%	9%	11%
Intelligence	13%	20%	28%	31%	8%	18%
Engineer/maintenance	10%	17%	28%	36%	10%	19%
Scientists/profession	16%	23%	29%	25%	6%	14%
Supply/procure/allied	11%	19%	27%	34%	9%	10%
Administration	12%	19%	25%	42%	10%	12%
All responses	12%	19%	26%	33%	9%	14%

Table D.23

Question 24: Responses by Current Joint Assignment

POSITION	OPINION OF THOSE WHO ANSWERED					NO ANSWER
	Strongly Agree	Agree	Neither Agree/Disagree	Disagree	Strongly Disagree	
On current JDAL	14%	21%	24%	33%	9%	10%
Not on JDAL	10%	16%	30%	34%	10%	18%
All responses	12%	19%	26%	33%	9%	14%

Question 25: my position/responsibility could be performed by an officer of another service.

Table D.24

Question 25: Responses by Grade

GRADE	OPINION OF THOSE WHO ANSWERED					NO ANSWER
	Strongly Agree	Agree	Neither Agree/Disagree	Disagree	Strongly Disagree	
O-3	30%	51%	5%	9%	4%	19%
O-4	29%	45%	5%	13%	8%	14%
O-5	28%	46%	5%	14%	8%	11%
O-6	33%	42%	3%	11%	10%	8%
O-7+	30%	37%	3%	13%	18%	17%
All	29%	46%	5%	12%	8%	13%

Table D.25

Question 25: Responses by Service

SERVICE	OPINION OF THOSE WHO ANSWERED					NO ANSWER
	Strongly Agree	Agree	Neither Agree/Disagree	Disagree	Strongly Disagree	
Army	28%	47%	5%	12%	7%	14%
Navy	33%	39%	5%	13%	9%	12%
Air Force	27%	49%	5%	12%	7%	13%
Marine Corps	33%	40%	5%	13%	9%	14%
All responses	29%	46%	5%	12%	8%	13%

Table D.26

Question 25: Responses by Skill Group

SKILL GROUP	OPINION OF THOSE WHO ANSWERED					NO ANSWER
	Strongly Agree	Agree	Neither Agree/Disagree	Disagree	Strongly Disagree	
Tactical operations	24%	42%	5%	18%	11%	11%
Intelligence	33%	48%	48%	9%	6%	17%
Engineer/maintenance	31%	52%	5%	8%	4%	18%
Scientists/profession	28%	48%	5%	13%	6%	13%
Supply/procure/allied	27%	47%	6%	13%	8%	9%
Administration	33%	45%	5%	11%	6%	12%
All responses	29%	46%	5%	12%	8%	13%

Question 26: my position/responsibility requires unique knowledge of my own service and could not be performed by an officer of another service.

Table D.27

Question 26: Responses by Grade

GRADE	OPINION OF THOSE WHO ANSWERED					NO ANSWER
	Strongly Agree	Agree	Neither Agree/Disagree	Disagree	Strongly Disagree	
O-3	4%	8%	9%	49%	30%	19%
O-4	8%	12%	9%	42%	28%	15%
O-5	8%	13%	8%	43%	27%	11%
O-6	10%	11%	6%	41%	32%	8%
O-7+	17%	13%	5%	33%	32%	17%
All	8%	12%	8%	43%	29%	13%

Table D.28

Question 26: Responses by Service

SERVICE	OPINION OF THOSE WHO ANSWERED					NO ANSWER
	Strongly Agree	Agree	Neither Agree/Disagree	Disagree	Strongly Disagree	
Army	7%	11%	9%	44%	28%	14%
Navy	10%	12%	8%	38%	32%	12%
Air Force	7%	12%	7%	47%	27%	13%
Marine Corps	11%	13%	8%	35%	33%	14%
All responses	8%	12%	8%	43%	29%	13%

Table D.29

Question 26: Responses by Skill Group

SKILL GROUP	OPINION OF THOSE WHO ANSWERED					NO ANSWER
	Strongly Agree	Agree	Neither Agree/Disagree	Disagree	Strongly Disagree	
Tactical operations	12%	17%	9%	41%	22%	11%
Intelligence	6%	9%	8%	45%	31%	17%
Engineer/maintenance	3%	9%	7%	49%	31%	18%
Scientists/profession	7%	9%	9%	45%	30%	14%
Supply/procure/allied	8%	13%	9%	44%	26%	9%
Administration	6%	11%	8%	42%	34%	12%
All responses	8%	12%	8%	43%	29%	13%

Question 27: morale problems will exist if joint duty credit is awarded for some positions in my immediate organization but not for others.

Table D.30

Question 27: Responses by Grade

GRADE	OPINION OF THOSE WHO ANSWERED					NO ANSWER
	Strongly Agree	Agree	Neither Agree/Disagree	Disagree	Strongly Disagree	
O-3	29%	36%	21%	11%	3%	19%
O-4	29%	35%	20%	13%	4%	14%
O-5	32%	36%	17%	11%	4%	11%
O-6	30%	37%	15%	14%	4%	8%
O-7+	29%	31%	14%	23%	3%	17%
All	30%	36%	18%	12%	4%	13%

Table D.31

Question 27: Responses by Service

SERVICE	OPINION OF THOSE WHO ANSWERED					NO ANSWER
	Strongly Agree	Agree	Neither Agree/Disagree	Disagree	Strongly Disagree	
Army	29%	37%	18%	13%	3%	14%
Navy	29%	34%	20%	12%	5%	12%
Air Force	31%	36%	18%	13%	3%	13%
Marine Corps	28%	35%	19%	11%	7%	14%
All responses	30%	36%	18%	12%	4%	13%

Table D.32

Question 27: Responses by Type Organization

ORGANIZATION	OPINION OF THOSE WHO ANSWERED					NO ANSWER
	Strongly Agree	Agree	Neither Agree/Disagree	Disagree	Strongly Disagree	
Joint Staff	47%	37%	10%	3%	3%	6%
Warfighting CINCs	32%	39%	17%	10%	2%	11%
Supporting CINCs	32%	38%	18%	10%	2%	15%
WHS/OSD	31%	36%	20%	10%	3%	7%
Defense agencies	26%	34%	23%	13%	4%	19%
In-service	13%	24%	18%	31%	14%	7%
All others	33%	36%	16%	12%	3%	13%
All responses	30%	36%	18%	12%	4%	13%

Table D.33

Question 27: Responses by Current Joint Assignment

POSITION	OPINION OF THOSE WHO ANSWERED					NO ANSWER
	Strongly Agree	Agree	Neither Agree/Disagree	Disagree	Strongly Disagree	
On current JDAL	33%	37%	17%	10%	3%	10%
Not on JDAL	25%	33%	21%	16%	5%	18%
All responses	30%	36%	18%	12%	4%	13%

Question 28: I expect my present assignment to contribute significantly to my performance in my future service assignments.

Table D.34

Question 28: Responses by Grade

GRADE	OPINION OF THOSE WHO ANSWERED					NO ANSWER
	Strongly Agree	Agree	Neither Agree/Disagree	Disagree	Strongly Disagree	
O-3	29%	41%	15%	9%	6%	19%
O-4	24%	37%	18%	12%	10%	15%
O-5	21%	37%	19%	13%	10%	11%
O-6	23%	38%	18%	12%	8%	8%
O-7+	35%	42%	14%	4%	5%	17%
All	24%	38%	18%	12%	9%	14%

Table D.35

Question 28: Responses by Service

SERVICE	OPINION OF THOSE WHO ANSWERED					NO ANSWER
	Strongly Agree	Agree	Neither Agree/Disagree	Disagree	Strongly Disagree	
Army	21%	38%	19%	13%	9%	15%
Navy	24%	33%	20%	11%	11%	12%
Air Force	26%	41%	16%	10%	7%	13%
Marine Corps	26%	35%	16%	13%	10%	14%
All responses	24%	38%	18%	12%	9%	14%

Table D.36

Question 28: Responses by Skill Group

SKILL GROUP	OPINION OF THOSE WHO ANSWERED					NO ANSWER
	Strongly Agree	Agree	Neither Agree/Disagree	Disagree	Strongly Disagree	
Tactical operations	22%	38%	18%	13%	10%	11%
Intelligence	24%	38%	19%	10%	9%	17%
Engineer/maintenance	24%	39%	18%	12%	7%	18%
Scientists/profession	21%	38%	17%	13%	11%	14%
Supply/procure/allied	28%	39%	17%	10%	7%	9%
Administration	24%	37%	18%	11%	9%	12%
All responses	24%	38%	18%	12%	9%	14%

Question 29: my service's interest in assigning officers to joint duty assignments has increased.

Table D.37

Question 29: Responses by Grade

GRADE	OPINION OF THOSE WHO ANSWERED					NO ANSWER
	Strongly Agree	Agree	Neither Agree/Disagree	Disagree	Strongly Disagree	
O-3	7%	28%	49%	10%	5%	20%
O-4	13%	35%	35%	11%	6%	15%
O-5	13%	39%	29%	12%	8%	11%
O-6	17%	46%	20%	11%	6%	9%
O-7+	36%	39%	15%	5%	6%	17%
All	13%	36%	33%	11%	7%	14%

Table D.38

Question 29: Responses by Service

SERVICE	OPINION OF THOSE WHO ANSWERED					NO ANSWER
	Strongly Agree	Agree	Neither Agree/Disagree	Disagree	Strongly Disagree	
Army	12%	39%	33%	10%	6%	15%
Navy	21%	42%	21%	10%	7%	12%
Air Force	10%	32%	39%	13%	7%	13%
Marine Corps	16%	37%	30%	10%	7%	14%
All responses	13%	36%	33%	11%	7%	14%

Table D.39

Question 29: Responses by Current Joint Assignment

POSITION	OPINION OF THOSE WHO ANSWERED					NO ANSWER
	Strongly Agree	Agree	Neither Agree/Disagree	Disagree	Strongly Disagree	
On current JDAL	14%	41%	27%	11%	7%	10%
Not on JDAL	11%	29%	41%	11%	6%	18%
All responses	13%	36%	33%	11%	7%	14%

Bibliography

99th Congress, First Session, *Defense Organization: The Need for Change*, Senate Print 99-86, Committee on Armed Services, United States Senate, October 16, 1985.

99th Congress, Second Session, *Reorganization of the Department of Defense, Hearings Before the Investigations Subcommittee of the Committee on Armed Services*, HASC No. 99-53, House of Representatives, 1987.

99th Congress, Second Session, *Department of Defense Reorganization Act of 1986*, P.L. 99-433, in United States Code Congressional and Administrative News, Volume 1, West Publishing Co., St. Paul, Minn., 1986.

99th Congress, Second Session, *Legislative History—Department of Defense Reorganization Act of 1986*, in United States Code Congressional and Administrative News, Volume 4, West Publishing Co., St. Paul, Minn., 1986.

100th Congress, First Session, *Department of Defense Authorization Act for Fiscal Year 1988*, P.L. 100-180, in United States Code Congressional and Administrative News, Volume 1, West Publishing Co., St. Paul, Minn., 1987.

100th Congress, Second Session, *National Defense Authorization Act for Fiscal Year 1989, Report of the Committee on Armed Services*, House of Representatives, Report 100-563, April 4, 1988.

100th Congress, Second Session, *Department of Defense Authorization Act for Fiscal Year 1989*, P.L. 100-456, in United States Code Congressional and Administrative News, Volume 1, West Publishing Co., St. Paul, Minn., 1988.

101st Congress, First Session, *Department of Defense Authorization Act for Fiscal Year 1990*, P.L. 101-189, in United States Code Congressional and Administrative News, Volume 1, West Publishing Co., St. Paul, Minn., 1989.

102nd Congress, Second Session, *Department of Defense Authorization Act for Fiscal Year 1990*, P.L. 102-484, in United States Code Congressional and Administrative News, Volume 2, West Publishing Co., St. Paul, Minn., 1992.

103rd Congress, First Session, *National Defense Authorization Act for Fiscal Year 1994, Conference Report to Accompany H.R. 2401*, House of Representatives, Report 103-357, November 10, 1993.

103rd Congress, First Session, *National Defense Authorization Act for Fiscal Year 1994, Report to the Committee on Armed Services*, Senate, Report 103-112, July 27, 1993.

Anderberg, Michael R., *Cluster Analysis for Applications*, Academic Press, San Diego, Calif., 1973.

Assistant Secretary of Defense (Force Management and Policy), *Joint Duty Positions Pertaining to Title IV of the DoD Reorganization Act*, Memorandum for the Under Secretaries of Defense, etc., Washington, D.C., December 4, 1986.

Assistant Secretary of Defense (Force Management and Personnel), *Report on the Study of Joint Officer Management Initiatives*, Washington, D.C., April 1990.

Assistant Secretary of Defense (Force Management and Personnel), *Restructured Joint Officer Program*, Memorandum for the Assistant Secretary of the Army (Manpower and Reserve Affairs), etc., Washington, D.C., November 18, 1991.

Assistant Secretary of Defense (Manpower, Reserve Affairs, and Logistics), *Assignment of Joint Tours of Duty*, Department of Defense Directive 1320.5, July 26, 1978.

Chairman of the Joint Chiefs of Staff, *Implementation of Title IV, DoD Reorganization Act*, Memorandum, CM-683-87, April 14, 1987.

Chairman of the Joint Chiefs of Staff, *Report on the Roles, Missions, and Functions of the Armed Forces of the United States*, CM-1584-93, February 1993.

Chairman of the Joint Chiefs of Staff, *Military Education Policy Document*, CM-1618-93, March 23, 1993.

Chairman of the Joint Chiefs of Staff, *Review of Promotion Selection Board Results by the Chairman of the Joint Chiefs of Staff*, Instruction, CJCSI 1330.02, January 7, 1994.

Coats, Lieutenant Colonel Julius E., *Joint Duty Prerequisite for Promotion to O-7 (Brigadier General)*, U.S. Army War College, Carlisle Barracks, Penn., March 13, 1989.

Committee on Armed Services, House of Representatives, *Report of the Panel on Military Education of the One Hundredth Congress*, First Session, Committee Print No. 4, April 21, 1989 [The Skelton Report].

Deputy Secretary of Defense, *Additional Guidelines for Administration of Joint Duty Assignment (JDA) Programs*, Memorandum for the Secretaries of the Military Departments, etc., Washington, D.C., August 22, 1988.

Deputy Secretary of Defense, *Additional Guidelines for the Implementation and Administration of the Joint Officer Management Programs*, Memorandum for the Secretaries of the Military Departments, etc., Washington, D.C., June 19, 1989.

Deputy Secretary of Defense, *Additional Guidelines for the Implementation of Title IV, DoD Reorganization Act of 1986*, Memorandum for Secretaries of the Military Departments, etc., Washington, D.C., February 4, 1988.

Deputy Secretary of Defense, *Career Guidelines and Oversight Procedures for Joint Specialty Officers and Other Officers Serving in Joint Duty Assignments*, Memorandum for Secretaries of the Military Departments, etc., Washington, D.C., July 22, 1987.

Deputy Secretary of Defense, *Revised Definitions for Dual-Hat and Cross-Department Joint Duty Assignments*, Memorandum for Secretaries of the Military Departments, etc., Washington, D.C., February 27, 1989.

Deputy Secretary of Defense, *Scientific and Technical Qualifications List*, Memorandum for the Secretaries of the Military Departments, etc., Washington, D.C., November 20, 1987.

Deputy Secretary of Defense, *Title IV, DoD Reorganization Act of 1986*, Memorandum for the Secretaries of the Military Departments, etc., Washington, D.C., May 21, 1987.

Fuller, Craig S., *The Navy and Jointness: No Longer Reluctant Partners?* Thesis, Naval Postgraduate School, Monterey, Calif., December 1991.

General Accounting Office, *Defense Personnel: Status of Implementing Joint Assignments for Military Leaders*, GAO/NSIAD-91-50BR, January 1991.

General Accounting Office, *Military Personnel: Designation of Joint Duty Assignments*, Report to Congressional Requestors, B-232940, February 1990.

Goldwater, Barry M., and Jack Casserly, *Goldwater*, Doubleday, New York, 1988 (especially Chapter 11, Duty-Honor-Country, pp. 334–361).

Hearings, House of Representatives, Committee on Armed Services, Investigations Subcommittee, Washington, D.C., May 1, 1987.

Joint Chiefs of Staff, *Joint Officer Management*, JCS Admin Pub 1.2, Washington, D.C., June 30, 1989.

Maze, Rick, "Lawmakers Reluctantly Endorse Joint Duty Waivers," *Air Force Times*, August 30, 1993, p. 9.

Office of the Assistant Secretary of Defense (Force Management and Personnel), "Report on the Study of Joint Officer Management Initiatives," draft, April 1990.

Savage, Colonel Dennis M., *Joint Duty Prerequisite for Promotion to General/Flag Officer*, U.S. Army War College, Carlisle Barracks, Penn., March 24, 1992.

Senate Armed Forces Committee, "Joint Officer Personnel Policy" and "Joint Duty Credit for Equivalent Duty in Operations Desert Shield/Desert Storm," from *the National Defense Authorization Act for Fiscal Year 1994*, Washington, D.C., July 27, 1993.

Syllogistics, Inc., *Analysis of Current and Alternative Provisions of Title IV: Joint Officer Personnel Policy*, Springfield, VA, May 1989.

Tomlinson, Major Paul L., "How Joint Officer Management Legislation Is Dividing Our Officer Corps," *Marine Corps Gazette*, October 1994, pp. 25–31.

Under Secretary of Defense (Personnel and Readiness), *Joint Duty Assignment Study (Interim Report)*, June 1994.

MR-574-JS

ISBN 0-8330-2302-0